For Judy and Richard,
"con amore",

David

22 II 97

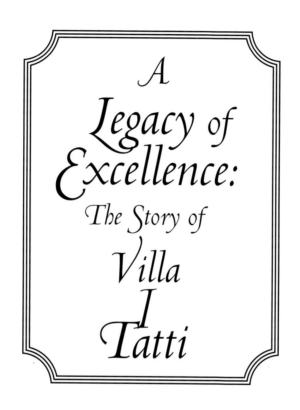

A
Legacy of
Excellence:
The Story of
Villa
I
Tatti

A Legacy of Excellence: The Story of Villa I Tatti

by

William Weaver

With Photographs by

David Finn

and

David Morowitz

Harry N. Abrams, Inc.

for Kazuo

The formal garden, or *giardino all'italiana*. Photo: David Finn

Above, and left:
The Departure of Coriolanus for Rome, details of city (left) and
landscape (above). The complete painting is shown on
pages 44–45. Photos: David Morowitz

Overleaf:
View of the villa and the formal garden, or *giardino
all'italiana*. Photo: I Tatti Archive

*I*t is hard to separate the life of a house from the life or lives of that house's inhabitants. And in the case of I Tatti, inhabited by the irresistibly fascinating and colorful Berensons, the task is virtually impossible. Still, in the pages that follow, I have tried to speak of Mary and Bernard Berenson only when their lives and the life of I Tatti were interlocked. Though a house called I Tatti had long existed where the villa now stands, the Villa I Tatti that most of the vast Berenson acquaintance knew and that continues to flourish today was, practically speaking, the creation of that singular couple. But, if they shaped the house, the house also shaped them. It made Mary into a chatelaine, whether she liked the role or not; and it made Berenson into the lord of that manor, the sage of that hermitage, the bait of that gilded trap.

The English writer Cyril Connolly, secretary as a young man to Mary's brother Logan Pearsall Smith, knew the Berensons and I Tatti well. In his delightful essay "The Grand Tour," written not long after Berenson's death and shortly before Harvard University had definitively established its Center for Italian Renaissance Studies in the villa bequeathed to it by that devoted member of the class of '87, Connolly, in expressing his grief at the death of a mentor, also described the house, saying: "[. . .] when we revisited I Tatti, Berenson's humanist sanctuary, it was pouring with rain. The great buff house with its magnificent library is now the property of the University of Harvard [. . .] The villa remains exactly as he left it, and I wandered through the empty rooms with their familiar objects, the Sienese paintings, the Chinese porphyry lion 'that had listened,' he once said, 'to so much good conversation,' even the array of thin gilded glasses that were used at his dinner parties, while I puzzled over the nature of existence.

"A man who lives to a great age and who acquires both fame and wisdom in the process, remaining for upwards of sixty years in the house which he has built, comes to seem more permanent and indestructible than many a landmark beside which we grew up. And suddenly he is there no longer; the order and ceremony with which he was surrounded prove an illusion and all the affectionate encouragement he gave to others, that too has vanished. However lovingly the home may be preserved, the personality evaporates with its discrimination and mischief; the perfect house becomes like a dead tooth; unswept, the cypress avenue grows older than its planter."

Lovingly tended, I Tatti certainly is (and the cypress avenue is carefully, regularly swept). Those who saw Berenson in his last years, almost translucent, small and trim and apparently weightless, seldom thought of him as physically indestructible. His continuing existence into his nineties seemed a triumph of the spirit, the life-force, over corporeal fragility. And that spirit

Berenson attributed this panel to the fifteenth-century Sienese Francesco di Giorgio Martini. This panel, showing a group of youths under a portico, is a fragment of a larger work. Pope-Hennessy agreed with the attribution, and dated the work between 1480 and 1490, connecting it with two other panels now in the Metropolitan Museum. More recent scholarship attributes the painting convincingly to Liberale da Verona. Photo: David Finn

has, indeed, proved beyond destruction; it survives in the order and—though altered—the ceremony that informs the life of Berenson's dwelling-place.

In his day, the library was one with the house; but the life of the house—known to many—overshadowed the intense life of the library, which was the sanctuary, to use Connolly's word, of its master and his disciples and a few of the house's many visitors. Today, the spirit surely lives on in the rooms of the house, where scholars gather around the Berenson table, where select visitors come to study the paintings, or in the garden, where the same scholars can relax and enjoy the enduring beauty that the Berensons, often painfully, brought into existence; but even more, that spirit lives on in the library, which continues to expand with vitality, as libraries must if they will remain vitalizing sources for their users.

Connolly last visited I Tatti at a peculiar moment of apparent stasis, while Harvard, the heir and the appointed keeper of the spirit, was still determining the future direction of the Center and selecting the people who would begin to guide the new institution along that path. If he were to come back today, more than thirty years later, it is safe to venture that he—lover of libraries, unabashed in his sustaining devotion to culture—would be impressed, favorably, by the condition of the beloved place. The match that Berenson lived to protect is now blazing bravely, nay merrily.

The brief book that follows is not meant as a work of scholarship. Though I spent many an enjoyable hour in Berenson's library, reading his letters to others, and many letters from others to him, not to mention Mary's outspoken, acute diaries, and memoirs of friends and what Berenson called friend-enemies, I have immensely profited—as I frankly and most gratefully admit—from the scholarly work of others. I have particularly made use of Ernest Samuels's indispensable two-volume biography *Bernard Berenson*, Nicky Mariano's endearing memoirs, *Forty Years with Berenson*, and Richard Dunn's biography of Geoffrey Scott, kindly made available to me in manuscript (now soon to be available also to others, in published form). My reading of autograph letters was, when possible, complemented by the various printed collections of Berenson's correspondence and by the selected letters and diaries of Mary Berenson in the volume *Mary Berenson, a self-portrait from her Letters and Diaries,* sensitively edited by her granddaughter Barbara Strachey with Jayne Samuels.

My own memories of Berenson are sadly few, but fortunately vivid; and my gratitude for his kindness in the busy life of his old age to an unknown, callow youth is enduring, as is my gratitude to the late Umberto Morra, who introduced that youth to I Tatti and its master. I am happy to recall here the affectionate hospitality of my friends Eleanor and Kenneth Murdock, when Kenneth was I Tatti's first resident director. The present director of the Center, Walter Kaiser, is the true begetter of this book, along with its publisher Paul Gottlieb. I thank them, as I also thank Professor Kaiser's assistant, my old friend Nelda Ferace, a pillar of efficiency and good humor, his secretary Susan Bates, and the entire staff of the villa. I Tatti's household, now headed

A rare photograph of Berenson laughing
(around 1935). In fact, he laughed frequently,
but tended to turn grave when confronted by
a camera. Courtesy, I Tatti Archive. Photo:
David Morowitz

by Liliana Ciullini, who has been a mainstay of I Tatti since Berenson's time, is an important part of the experience of the villa. Other members of Liliana's family worked there most of their lives; the late (and excellent) cook Nello Nardi was succeeded by his wife Luisa, who prepared meals together with Lilia Sarti, wife of Gino, one of the three Sarti brothers, who worked on the farms for decades. The devotion of the staff, and their unbroken years of service, are a moving testimony to the spirit of the place.

My thanks are due also to I Tatti's former gardener, Alessandro Tombelli; to the library staff, Assunta Pisani, Anna Terni (who has been at I Tatti since 1949); and to the curator of the Fototeca and the Berenson Archive, Fiorella Superbi Gioffredi, who was born on the estate, knows its every cranny, and shares her knowledge freely with scholars and visitors. I am especially indebted also to her father, Geremia Gioffredi, who kindly agreed to spend a memorable afternoon with me and my tape-recorder, recalling old and turbulent times.

Since 1980 the Center has had an important office in the United States, first in New York, then in Cambridge. From there, Alexa Mason, assistant director for external relations, has supplied me with cordial and exhaustive answers to many pesky questions, also earning my sincere gratitude.

W. W.
Monte San Savino

The front driveway to the villa. Photo: David Finn

1

*T*he three gardeners are the first to arrive at the villa, while the three farmers are, invisibly, already at work in the surrounding fields. In this season—it is June, and the weather is turning warm—the flowers and shrubs need their ration of water early. The head gardener Margrit Freivogel has to spend much of the morning creating new flower arrangements—or refreshing yesterday's—for the dozens of vases that grace nearly all the rooms of the villa. Outside, the potted lemons may be thirsty, the graveled paths will need raking, and, on a less aesthetic but equally satisfying level, there will be some vegetables to gather for the communal lunch. The young, blond Margrit is often there by seven.

For almost a century, the Villa I Tatti at Settignano has repeated certain rituals, as season follows season, as one set of visitors succeeds another. From 1900 until his death in 1959, the occupant and motive force of the villa was the connoisseur-writer-aesthete Bernard Berenson. After his death, by the terms of his will, the house and its contents, the art collection, the elaborate garden, and—most important—the copious library and photograph collection were bequeathed to Harvard University, which set up the Center for Italian Renaissance Studies.

Externally, the villa and its grounds look much as they did when Berenson died. Guarded by stately cypresses, protected by a discreet wall, I Tatti maintains its reserve, its scholarly silence. Inside, too, many things are unchanged: most of the pictures hang in the places assigned them by their collector; the Egyptian cat still sits erect on the sixteenth century wooden *cassone* in the main hall; luncheon is still served at one, and tea at four-thirty. Life is scheduled, regulated as it was in the time of Berenson, whose days at I Tatti went by in an organized division of work, reading, and conversation with the never-ending procession of visitors.

At nine A. M. the sturdy double gates at number 22 Via di Vincigliata, Settignano, are shut. In fact, they will remain shut all day, opening only when a button is pressed inside the nearby building, after a closed circuit screen has been consulted. But at that hour, the Biblioteca Berenson is prepared to begin its working day. Patrizia Carella is at the reception table, where the telephone has started ringing, the head librarian Assunta Pisani is in her office, as the rest of the library staff are at their tasks.

Gradually, the fellows and visiting scholars begin to gather. Some arrive by car, waiting at the gate to be buzzed in; others, on foot, come up or down from I Tatti's dépendances, the Villa Papiniana higher up the hill, the Villino on the other side of the road, about fifty meters towards the hamlet of San Martino a Mensola, where still more are housed. A few hardy spirits take the bus from Florence and trudge up the winding, but fortunately shaded road.

Opposite:
The main entry hall, looking east, with the Egyptian cat on the *cassone* at right, where outgoing letters were left by guests for posting by the I Tatti staff.
Photo: David Morowitz

On entering, one or two may stop in the sunny atrium to collect mail, study the bulletin board, or glance through the Italian papers or the *International Herald-Tribune*, left on a convenient sill. Many of the library's familiars head straight for their usual spots, the studies or tables where the books they are using or the documents they are consulting are in place, awaiting them. In the Fototeca—the archive of three hundred thousand photographs begun by Berenson and his wife in the last century—art historians may be consulting photographs of now-lost or war-destroyed paintings, or of accessible paintings now restored out of any close likeness to the photographs—including even some old picture post cards—that the Berensons painstakingly found and bought or commissioned many decades ago. Though the Berensons were indefatigable travelers (Bernard made an extended visit to Southern Italy and to North Africa in 1955, when he was in his ninetieth year), Berenson was one of the first scholars to realize and exploit the importance of photographs in studying and assessing works of art. His successors have learned his lesson, and the Fototeca—under the direction of Berenson-trained Fiorella Superbi Gioffredi—is as sought out by art historians as the famous library itself.

There is no such thing as a typical day at the Biblioteca Berenson, though many of its users—the villa's Fellows, in particular—come back day after day all during the year. And former Fellows, even after their official stay is long ended, retain their privileges and are always welcome to pay a visit, to conduct research and simply to share and enliven the villa's luncheons. Other scholars, too, perhaps in Florence briefly, may well feel the need to pay the library a visit, to check a reference in a rare or unique volume.

On a recent morning, there was a sudden influx of landscape architects and garden historians, as the Georgetown University Center, at the nearby Villa Le Balze in Fiesole, was sponsoring an all-day conference on the architect Cecil Pinsent, co-creator (with Geoffrey Scott) of I Tatti's gardens and of the gardens and the villa of Le Balze, as well as some other Tuscan showplaces. In the big reading room of the library, Scott's biographer Richard Dunn was going through a thick stack of his subject's letters. In a lateral reading room, at one table, the Italian architectural historian Giorgio Galletti (curator of the Boboli Gardens at the Palazzo Pitti) was looking at Pinsent's papers, sharing them with the English garden writer Ethne Clarke, seated at his side.

During coffee break, in the nearby Granaio (the former granary of the home farm), recently converted into a comfortable, spacious common room, with facilities for making coffee and tea, the scholars shared their information with a newcomer, a writer working on the Berensons, generously pointing out this or that perhaps ignored source. The visiting writer had found, stuck into a volume of Mary Berenson's tart and forthright diaries, two eighty-year-old snapshots of Mary with the young Geoffrey. Scott's biographer Dunn flushed with pleasure and hurried back to the main library to inspect the welcome find.

For decades, the ancient Egyptian cat in the entrance hall of the villa has welcomed visitors to I Tatti. In her autobiography Iris Origo, lifelong friend of Berenson, wrote: "For many years I felt the house's presiding genius to be the first object one encountered on entering, an Egyptian cat seated on a trecento *cassone* in the hall—elegant, inscrutable, irresistibly attractive. It was only when you put out your hand to stroke it, that you discovered it to be made of bronze." Photo: David Finn

By late morning, the photocopying machines are working at full tilt; and at most of the catalogue computers—the whole library has been professionally put on line—researchers are busily tapping out their enquiries. Some of them work right through the lunch hour, while the Fellows and the villa's guests file out—in fair weather—for an *aperitivo* under the cypress and ilex trees, in the restful shade of their complementary umbrellas at the western end of the villa. Vermouths and Campari are on offer, but most of the scholars prudently stick to tomato juice, spicing it perhaps with a dash of Tabasco.

It is harder to resist the red wine from I Tatti's own farm—the villa owns some seventy-five acres, a reasonable patch of Tuscany—where grapes and olive trees provide not only wine for the scholars' table but delicious oil for

The eastern side of the villa, with
the front door and the arches (designed
by Pinsent) of the kitchen courtyard.
Photo: David Finn

Left:
The veteran gardener Bruno Ciullini
(member of a large family with
long-time I Tatti associations) and
the British-trained Alessandro Tombelli,
who supervised much of the garden's
renovation in the early 1990s. After
retiring as head gardener in 1995, he
has remained a consultant.
Photo: I Tatti Archive.

their salad, also produced on the estate. As in Berenson's own day, the table-talk can range from Florentine (or academic) gossip to the proper collocation of a Bolognese altarpiece or the Tuscan use of the word *corpo* ("body") to mean "stomach," a curious local metonymy.

After lunch, if the sun is shining, even the most dedicated academic might grant himself a half-hour to stroll in the garden, now—thanks to a generous donor, Lila Acheson Wallace—brought to a splendor that it seldom had even in its heyday. Actually, this *is* its heyday, in the opinion of many. During Berenson's last years, the garden was neglected, and in the first years

I Tatti's fruitful potted lemon trees, which winter in the Limonaia and decorate the garden during spring and summer. Photo: David Morowitz

after his death, the new proprietor of I Tatti—Harvard University—had other, more pressing matters to deal with.

Some of the younger Fellows and some members of the staff may skip coffee and repair to the Limonaia, the long, low structure on a kind of terrace-shelf that divides the sloping garden. Drinks or tea were sometimes served there in Berenson's time; since then it has been also used for large, informal lunches, and—after recent improvements—it can serve as a lecture hall (though its original inhabitants, the potted lemon trees, still use it as their winter home). At one end of the hangar-like room, a ping-pong table has been set up, and the members of the informal team that has come into unprogrammed existence may work out a little before returning to their more serious tasks.

The library continues its quiet, but intense activity during the afternoon

The Limonaia, with some of I Tatti's potted lemon trees already installed for the winter. Photo: David Finn

hours, until tea summons the Fellows again to the shady corner of the garden. In colder weather, they gather in the living room (or music room, as Berenson called it, as it once housed a piano). There tea is served—with homemade cookies provided by the zealous kitchen staff—under the great Sassetta triptych, as it was served in Berenson's day to his steady stream of guests.

At six, the library closes (the Fellows can remain at their work until ten). Often, however, the intellectual life of the villa continues. At regular intervals, in the great reading room, there are lectures, followed by a reception. Visiting authorities on various aspects of Renaissance culture may elaborate on their specialty: Harvard's Dante Della Terza may speak about Dante, or the fellows in residence may report on the progress of their investigations.

The exact date of Berenson's decision to bequeath his villa, his library, and his works of art, to Harvard is not known, but it was fairly early in his own residence there. As a young immigrant, brilliant but without means, he had basked in the enlightened glow of the great university, and had retained a filial attachment to it. He kept in touch, for the rest of his life, with many of his distinguished classmates—George Santayana, Charles Augustus Strong, among them—and some of his old professors, including William James, visited him in Florence, where he could turn the tables, and act as their instructive cicerone. His beloved sister Rachel married the Harvard philosopher Ralph Barton Perry.

Harvard was not as eager to receive the demanding gift as its donor was to give it, but the university finally accepted. One person very much opposed to the idea was Mary Berenson. Mother of two children from an unhappy first marriage, by the 1930s she was a grandmother, and—despite Berenson's

Berenson (second from right) during his Harvard days. The women, who are unidentified, may have been members of his family. Courtesy, I Tatti Archive. Photo: David Morowitz

notorious dislike of children—she was anxious for her descendants to inherit, though she and Berenson had generously provided for them, as Berenson had also unstintingly taken care of his own family over many years.

Shortly before his death in 1995, the art historian and Berenson disciple Sir John Pope-Hennessy recalled that, from his earliest visits to the house, in the late 1930s, he had heard Berenson speak enthusiastically of his plans for I Tatti after his death. "He didn't talk about it frequently, however, because Mrs. Berenson was often present, and she did not approve of the plan." Mary Berenson once contemptuously described Bernard's vision of "a lay monastery of leisurely culture" as amounting to no more than "a wayside inn for loafing scholars."

Asked if the atmosphere of the villa had changed much since Berenson's death, Pope-Hennessy said, "No, it is much the same." Other frequenters of the Berenson household would probably disagree, for—as opposed to the library—the residence has undergone a few significant changes: former servants' quarters have been turned into studies for senior Fellows, Berenson's

Above:
The *giardino pensile* ("hanging garden"),
at wisteria time, before the recent restoration. Photo: David Finn

Right:
The *giardino pensile* from the library.
The urns, in Tuscan *pietra serena*, lovely
but friable, were replaced by newly
carved ones in 1993. Designed by
Pinsent, the urns correspond to the
wooden urns in the new library and the
proportionately smaller ones in the small
library, making a visual continuum
between indoors and outdoors. Photo:
David Finn

Above:
Grapes in late summer in the I Tatti vineyard. Photo: David Morowitz

Right:
A few years ago the Director of the Center set up an informal competition for the design of a label for the villa's wine. There were forty entries—some from the children of the household, others from employees—to be judged by the Director Walter Kaiser, Gabriele Geier (an I Tatti friend and benefactor), and a visiting scholar. The winner was the artist Don Campbell. His design was based on a pattern of superimposed circles made by wet wineglasses. Photo: David Morowitz

private study has become a small, more informal sitting-room where the resident director can receive. But some of the household staff were already at the villa in Berenson's day, and among certain local families there is a long tradition of working at I Tatti. Thus even a crowded Fellows' lunch never has the sense of an institutional meal; the Fellows and their friends instinctively feel that they are valued, privileged guests in an elegant country home, where hospitality has been practiced and prized for almost a century.

In the library, though it is visited by hundreds of scholars in the space of a year, the same reverent sense of devotion to art and to learning still reigns. In the reading rooms, the loudest sound is likely to be the turning of a page. And in the granary-turned-common room, the serious, informed talk is often leavened with jesting and laughter—a sound that always delighted the former master.

The complex polyptych painted by Sassetta between 1437 and 1444 for the church of San Francesco at Borgo Sansepolcro was dismembered in the early nineteenth century; the various surviving components are now divided among the Louvre, the National Gallery in London, the Condé Museum in Chantilly, the Berlin Museum, the Pushkin Museum in Moscow, and other collections. A few elements have been lost. Berenson bought the central panel of St. Francis in ecstasy and the two lateral panels of St. John the Baptist (right) and Blessed Ranieri Rasini (left) around 1902, supposedly from a cabinetmaker, who was about to use the wood in the construction of fake antiques. Formerly attributed to Piero della Francesca or Beato Angelico, the three panels were recognized by Berenson as the work of Stefano di Giovanni, known as Sassetta, a painter then in the process of being rediscovered. Berenson, a motive figure in that process, published his monograph on Sassetta, *A Sienese Painter of the Franciscan Legend*, in 1909. The essay represents some of Berenson's most affecting prose, particularly the pages devoted to his own Franciscan Sassettas, which dominate the living room, or "music room" as it was called in Berenson's day. Photo: David Finn

The Chapel. Photo: David Finn

Opposite:
Berenson acquired this Neroccio di Bartolomeo Landi (Siena 1447–1500) from a London dealer in 1911. It portrays Saints Dominic, Francis, and Bonaventure (or Benedict) appearing before St. Catherine of Siena. The architecture, suggesting the works of Leon Battista Alberti, frames the learned saint, as the three monk-saints hand her a spray of lilies. Photo: David Morowitz

2

*I*n the spring of 1900, Bernhard Berenson (as he then spelled his first name) and Mary Costelloe, his companion of about a decade, decided finally to marry and to live together under the same roof. Mary's first husband, the Anglo-Irish barrister and political figure Frank Costelloe, had died the previous March; and his widow would now be able, after this decent interval, to legitimize the relationship that dominated her life. "We took a new villa," she wrote from Florence on 7 May, to her less-than-approving mother in London. A few weeks later, to the same correspondent she mentioned the villa by name: "Busy at I Tatti," she wrote on 9 June; and four days

View from the Villa Papiniana, with the Villino in the foreground, I Tatti in the middle ground, and Poggio Gherardo in the distance. Photo: David Finn

after that, thoroughly engaged in the villa's decoration, triumphantly returning from a bargaining expedition to the house of a wily farmer, she informed her mother that the "fireplace for the sala is ours."

On 30 October, though much work remained to be done, there was a grand celebratory meal at the villa for the forty workmen engaged in refurbishing it, but shortly afterwards Mary had to record in her diary that she had run out of funds to pay the hands. Ever resilient and resourceful, she scraped more money together, and work was virtually completed by Christmas. On

27 December, after some tedious untangling of bureaucratic red tape, Berenson and Mary were married in a civil ceremony in Florence's Palazzo Vecchio; two days later, in the chapel of I Tatti—a simple little structure standing against the garden wall near the gate—a religious ceremony took place. Though both Bernhard and Mary had been converted to Catholicism at some point in their lives, both had long stopped practicing it; the wedding was more of a social formality than a sacred ceremony. But, now doubly wedded, they moved that same day into the villa which would remain their home for the rest of their lives.

They were a strange pair. At Christmas, 1900, when they moved into their house, the Jewish, Lithuanian-born, Harvard-educated Berenson was thirty-five; Mary, originally a Philadelphia Quaker, was a year older, with two small daughters, who lived in England with Mary's resolute mother. Overcoming his humble origins, Berenson had already won an enviable international reputation as an art expert, or connoisseur, as he would have preferred to be called; he was almost single-handedly responsible for making connoisseurship a recognized profession. Having lived scandalously in sin—though in rigorously separate establishments—the now respectably-married couple had outgrown the passion of their early years together but continued to share an often tense partnership, infrangible, yet fraught with reciprocal, usually acknowledged infidelities. They were not so much husband and wife as they were accomplices. By this time, Mary had published a number of articles and at least one book, and she collaborated—or combatted—with her husband on his work, criticizing his prose style, scornfully cutting self-indulgent passages. Later she helped him with the endless revision and extension of his famous "lists" of Italian paintings, giving their whereabouts and establishing their attribution. She kept notebooks full of observations, sometimes supplemented by simple sketches of altarpieces or chapels in out-of-the-way churches. Her letters often included descriptions of art works along with gossip about artists, collectors, and rival experts.

Though Mary had a small regular competency and Berenson's expertises (and commissions on sales of art works) would soon begin to generate considerable income, the two were perpetually hard up, partly because of Mary's incurable extravagance and her generosity to her family, partly because of Berenson's then equally incurable mania for acquisition as well as his undeniable love of comfort, even luxury. Though he later refused to consider himself a collector (and his personal collection was relatively small), Berenson never stopped amassing photographs—his Fototeca comprised 300 thousand items at his death—and books (he left a library of 50 thousand volumes). By the time he established himself at I Tatti, fellow connoisseurs and students were already asking permission to consult his library and photographs.

A piece of land called I Zatti is recorded in a document dating from the 11th century, and there may have been some kind of house on the property even then. By the early 18th century the owners were the powerful but litigious Alessandrini family; their coat-of-arms features a two-headed sheep, symbolizing the family's division. The Janus-like animal, its heads cantankerously facing in opposite directions, can be seen in the arch near the kitchen courtyard of the villa today and, more prominently, over the door of the family chapel, built—as an inscription confirms—in 1724.

The Berensons must have known I Tatti long before they took the lease on it. At the turn of the century, one of their protégés, the English painter and sometime-dealer James Kerr-Lawson, was living with his wife in the so-called Casa di Boccaccio, in the vicinity of I Tatti. And at the top of the hill, in the great castle of Vincigliata, lived their landlord, the rich, elderly English eccentric Temple Leader, whose residence, "restored" to Victorian medieval gloom, was described by Henry James, in *Italian Hours*. "Vincigliata," he wrote, "is a product of the millions, the leisure and the eccentricity, I suppose people say, of an English gentleman, Mr. Temple Leader ... in the dusky courts and chambers of the present elaborate structure this impassioned archaeologist must have buried a fortune. He has, however, the compensation of feeling that he has erected a monument which, if it is never to stand a feudal siege, may encounter at least some critical overhauling ... he has kept throughout such rigid terms with his model that the result is literally uninhabitable to degenerate moderns."

The tenant who had preceded the Berensons in I Tatti was equally indifferent to the latest conveniences; and a good deal of basic work had to be done. Though I Tatti was—and is—called a villa, it was hardly more than an overgrown farmhouse, not in the same league with the true, grander villas nearby, whose owners were—or soon became—part of the Berensons' circle of acquaintance. The doughty, and virtually legendary, Janet Ross lived at nearby Poggio Gherardo; a widow, she had taken in her orphaned niece, Caroline ("Lina") Duff-Gordon (later Waterfield) as her companion. Both women became particularly close friends of Mary's. In later years, Lina's children regularly participated in the delightful and elaborate picnics, parties, and games that Mary organized for her grandchildren. Berenson, whose dislike of the young mellowed only in his last years, tended to be elsewhere on these festive occasions.

In the other direction lay the Medicean Villa Gamberaia, rented by the exotic Princess Giovanna Ghyka, whose companion, Miss Florence Blood, became a member of the Tatti clan, a striking, if sometimes reluctant component of the numerous, long-established, ingrown and sometimes quarrelsome English and American Florentine colony, the *anglo-beceri* as native Florentines called them (*becero* — literally "boor" — is the dialect word with which some Florentines define themselves).

In Florence there was a noble, centuries-old tradition of foreign—especially Anglophone—settlers, lovers of the arts, often moneyed eccentrics. The child Mozart, visiting the city in 1770, encountered the grand dilettante Milord Cowper (and probably his more famous countryman Sir Horace Mann); and, a few years later, a local youth, Luigi Cherubini, showing musical

An inscription on the back of this tiny (18 x 14.3 cm) panel of Christ on the Cross and the Symbols of the Passion testifies that it was painted by Lorenzo Lotto and finished on Good Friday "at the hour of the Passion of our Lord Jesus Christ." The writer, a contemporary of the artist, does not give the year, but Berenson placed it around 1532. The work was given to Berenson by his Florentine friend Count Alessandro Contini Bonacossi, who no doubt knew Berenson's early (1895) and still magisterial monograph on Lotto. Photo: David Finn

promise, was also helped on his way by Earl Cowper. He lived in the Villa Palmieri at San Domenico, inhabited a century later by Violet Paget—the English writer known as Vernon Lee—who often received and quarreled with Berenson there. In the 19th century, settlers like the Trollopes, the Brownings, Ouida (who devoted a whole novel to a cruel caricature of Janet Ross),the popular writers Mrs. Oliphant and Miss Mitford confirmed and expanded the tradition; and first their presence, then their legend attracted many other foreign settlers. Today, a plaque at the bottom of Via di Vincigliata—the road that leads up to the gate of I Tatti—recalls some of the famous past residents of the little area; among the foreign names is that of Mark Twain, whom the Berensons met and disliked.

Many of Florence's temporary residents were hard-working, professional writers, like Twain and like Vernon Lee. Others lived an ingrown life of cultivated leisure, entertaining one another and offering hospitality to transient stars, who might range from Henry James to Queen Victoria. A few—Mrs. Browning among them—became passionately interested in the Italian political situation or in the contemporary Italian culture. But many lived in Florence as they might live in Buffalo or Aberdeen; and they did not always take the trouble to perfect their command of Italian, beyond the limited vocabulary of housekeeping and locomotion. Mary Berenson, typically, spoke clumsy, heavily-accented Italian for all the half-century or more that she lived in Tuscany. Her imperfect command of the language, however, did not diminish her wit or curb her acidity.

I Tatti is just visible from the much grander Poggio Gherardo, the imposing crenellated residence which, tradition has it, Boccaccio used as the setting for the opening three days of the *Decameron*. The Berensons exchanged regular visits with the formidable Mrs. Ross—eventually known to I Tatti's residents as "Aunt Janet" (as she was called by her niece Lina) — wife of a banker and author of several books on Tuscany, including the simple and excellent guide to cooking vegetables, *Leaves from a Tuscan Kitchen*, still happily in print. When the never-ceasing work on I Tatti became particularly cumbersome, Mary would sometimes take refuge at Poggio.

The tradition of I Tatti's hospitality began as soon as the Berensons moved in: the first guests—invited immediately, somewhat to the master's dismay—were Mary's brother, the fastidious writer and aesthete Logan Pearsall Smith, and her two little daughters, Rachel ("Ray") and Karin. The fact that stairs had yet to be carpeted, many doors refused to close properly, and the electrical and hydraulic systems still created daily difficulties did not stop the Berensons from encouraging people to come, nor did it discourage others, uninvited, from arriving. For weeks on end, Mary's diaries provide a dazzling list of guests: for lunch, for tea, for dinner. Sometimes a guest would arrive for the earliest meal, then stay for the other two. And the bell was constantly rung by vendors of "art"; Mary had to turn away dozens of would-be salesmen, hawking presumed Giottos and Michelangelos.

For the most part, the visitors to I Tatti were not Italian. It was not until some time later that, through Vernon Lee, Berenson met the ubiquitous Carlo Placci, a dilettante writer of independent means who made it his business to know everyone, including—as the Queen of Belgium once said—"the unknown soldier." A social catalyst, he made a point of introducing his friends to one another. And he was responsible for positively launching Berenson among the aristocrats of Florence. An opinionated bachelor, Placci often disagreed with Berenson, especially about religion and politics. Their friendship finally suffered a permanent rift when the arch-Catholic, hotly patriotic Placci enthusiastically embraced Fascism.

In the early years, neither Bernhard (who became Bernard at the time of World War I) nor Mary stayed in the villa on a permanent basis. Mary made frequent visits to England to see her family, while Berenson regularly sought out the intellectual stimulation of Paris—where he became friends with Henri Bergson, met Matisse, Gide, Proust—and the social excitement of St. Moritz, with its beautiful, stylish women and its elegant night life. There he even went to a fancy-dress ball, dressed as an Arab prince. Frequently, with Mary accompanying him, he traveled widely to study out-of-the-way works of art, from crumbling, icy rural Italian churches to baronial halls, hung with Italian masterworks, often grandiosely misattributed.

At the time he moved into I Tatti, Berenson had already laid the basis of his fame, establishing his authority with books like *The Venetian Painters of the Renaissance*, *The Florentine Painters of the Renaissance*, *The Central Italian Painters of the Renaissance* (all with their invaluable lists of attributed paintings); his monograph on Lorenzo Lotto, which brought this long-neglected painter to the attention of art-lovers, had appeared in 1895 and had already been reprinted. His first series of essays, *The Study and Criticism of Italian Art*, came out in 1901, as he was settling into his house, where he continued his enormous labor on *The Drawings of the Florentine Painters,* which John Murray issued in two magnificent volumes in 1903. After *The North Italian Painters of the Renaissance*, published in 1907, the pace of Berenson's writing slackened; much of his time was devoted to the revision and extension of his four books on Renaissance painters, all of which went through several editions. Only with the second World War, and his temporary isolation and immobility, did his writing enter a productive and satisfying phase of sunset brilliance; he then published volumes of diaries and autobiography, studies of Caravaggio and Piero della Francesca. He died more admired as a writer than he had ever been.

In all this, I Tatti—slowly, painfully created from the original modest rural house—was a constant. In his periods of travel, away from his books and photographs and his secretary-critic-editor-goad Mary, Berenson could do practically no writing. So the works of his later career were nearly all associated with the house at Settignano and, in the last decades, with his summer refuges in Vallombrosa, an hour away in the cool woods of the Apennines.

Left:
Vincenzo Foppa, *Madonna and Child with Music-Making Angels.*
Photo: David Finn

Above:
This unidentified Franciscan saint was painted in the early years of the fourteenth century either by Giotto or by one of his very close collaborators. Berenson was convinced the panel was the work of the master himself, and a number of authorities agree with him. As Berenson wrote of Giotto: "He aims at types which both in face and figure are simple, large-boned, and massive—types, that is to say, which in actual life would furnish the most powerful stimulus to the tactile imagination. Obliged to get the utmost out of his rudimentary light and shade, he makes the scheme of colour of the lightest that his contrasts may be of the strongest."
Photo: David Finn

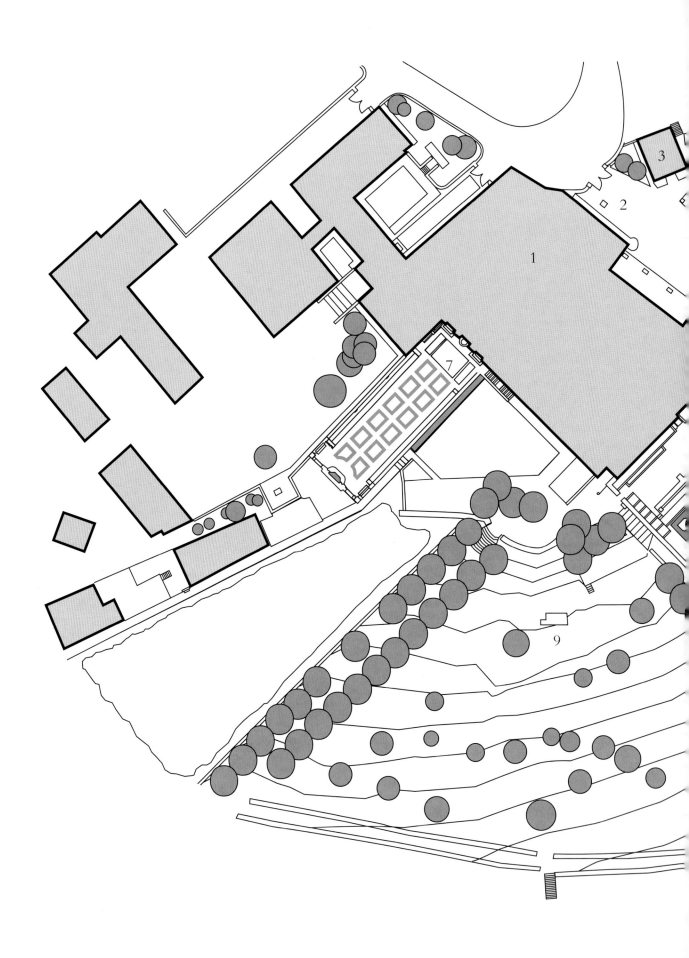

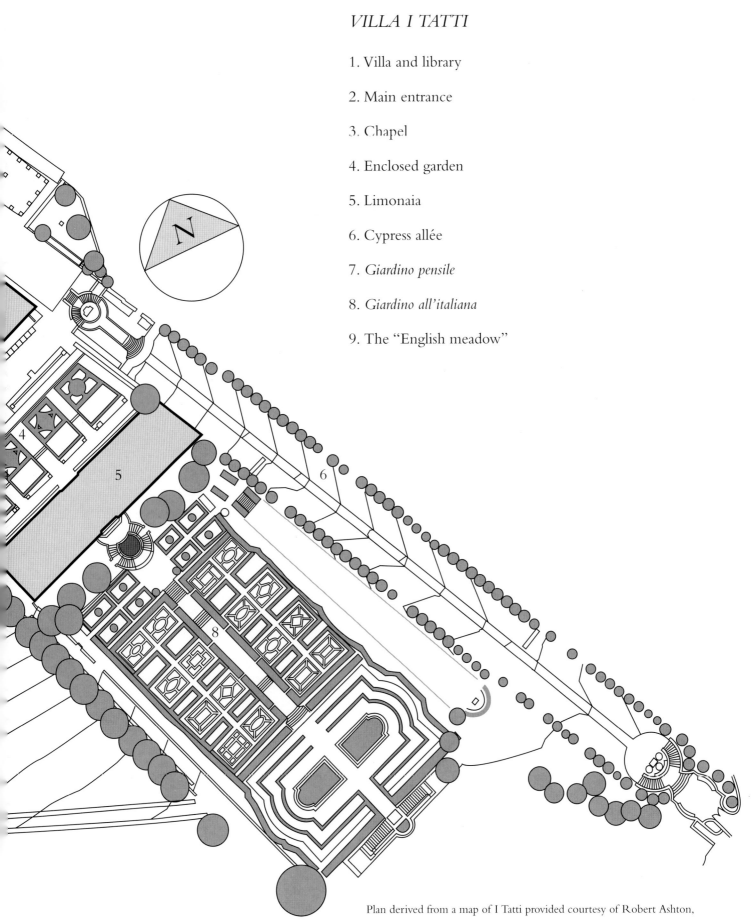

VILLA I TATTI

1. Villa and library

2. Main entrance

3. Chapel

4. Enclosed garden

5. Limonaia

6. Cypress allée

7. *Giardino pensile*

8. *Giardino all'italiana*

9. The "English meadow"

Plan derived from a map of I Tatti provided courtesy of Robert Ashton, CAD Centre, De Montfort University, U.K.

Above:
In Rome at the beginning of the century, visiting an antique market, Berenson found this Gentile da Fabriano *Madonna and Child*. Berenson called Gentile the first great Umbrian master and praised his "glowing vivacity of fancy." Photo: David Finn

Opposite:
The Berenson collection has two works by the fifteenth-century Florentine Neri di Bicci, a charming oblong predella panel of the *Nativity* and this graceful, delicate *Madonna*, who, in the company of St. Lawrence kneeling on his grille, is adoring a lively Christ child. Photo: David Morowitz

In the spring of 1903, when the Berensons had been living in I Tatti three years and had already set their own seal on it, their nonegenarian land-lord, Temple Leader, died. Childless, he left everything to his grand-nephew, the third Lord Westbury, a notorious profligate, who wanted to raise some cash by selling the Settignano property. In no position to buy, the Berensons persuaded him to grant them a new lease. Though Bernhard's income was steadily growing, so were his family responsibilites, and Mary's extrava-gances—like his own—tended to increase with their income, though not always proportionately.

The situation seemed precarious again in 1906, and during that spring and summer Mary and Bernhard inspected several other villas, possible new homes. Finally, through a friend, the powerful American banker Henry Can-non, resident of the grand Villa La Doccia in nearby Fiesole, they were able to procure a loan on advantageous terms, and in November 1907, Mary went

to see the new landlord's agent "and offered 140,000 francs for this house and the two poderi [farms]. He said he would transmit the offer to Lord Westbury. Full of hope."

On 14 December, Mary could write in her diary: "Well—!! This house is ours at last. The factor came today to tell us that Lord Westbury has accepted our offer of £135.000 plus the "stime" [estimated value] of cattle, horses, *arnesi*, [tools] etc., wh. comes to another £5000. This settles a long-standing anxiety, for it was so awful to think of being turned out at the end of our time, in May 1909 . . . The servants got up a little 'festa' in the evening with endless candles and flowers in the dining room. I think they are all pleased . . ."

The next day's entry is a kind of postscript: "It was absolutely pleasant to wake up in *our own house*. Everything seemed more delightful, and I was very happy."

Early in the new year, "we walked . . . and surveyed with complacency the limits of our domain, wishing, however, that they were even larger! Bernhard wd. like to buy the whole woods!"

In March, Logan returned and took a walk "over the place" with Mary, to suggest plans for the garden and other improvements. And a few days later—on 10 March—Mary could write: "Signed the contract for this place and paid the money—139000 francs—5000 for the cattle and *arnesi* etc. and nearly 6000 for the registration fees etc. It comes to six thousand pounds—wh. we have borrowed at 6% £360, as against £80 we used to pay for rent. It is a big increase. Of course the place brings us something, but then we have taxes and improvements. I think it is a clear £200 more a year to spend. But anyhow we now own the place."

3

Arresting in its dark and dramatic bustle, this small (31 × 20 cm.) panel of *The Crucifixion* by the Ferrarese Ercole de' Roberti is propped, with some other works, against a damasked wall over a Renaissance credenza. Berenson acquired the picture rather late, in 1922, when his collection was largely formed. The attribution has been disputed. Photo: David Finn

For the first alterations at I Tatti, after they moved in at the beginning of 1901, Mary and Bernhard had relied largely on their own taste and on the help of local workmen. There seems to have been no general plan, and no drawings or written instructions survive. From later diaries and letters of Mary's, it emerges that there was only one bath, the house was without electricity, and there was no telephone.

But in 1909, now that the house belonged to them, both Berensons felt that a more drastic and ennobling renovation was necessary. On the most practical plane, a second bathroom had to be added on the upper floor, which meant extending running water to that floor as well. Electricity would also have to be installed. But, not content with these mundane improvements, Mary argued that, while they were about it, they should build a whole new kitchen in the rear, with "a scullery, pantry, and—wine cellar! — a servants' hall, larder, ironing room, and butler's pantry, as well as a big cupboard for sweets and fruits, etc. off the dining room (the present kitchen), and two bedrooms and a bathroom on the top floor. So there would be room for endless parties of Young People such as I delight in." Bernhard—almost certainly not informed of these plans for endless parties of Young People—insisted that he needed space for a proper library, which would have to be added on to the residence.

As part of their agreement with Lord Westbury, they would also be entitled to their own key to the little artificial lake in the Vincigliata woods, where Mary was fond of bathing and of inviting guests to do the same. Later, she memorably described Gertrude Stein's immersion into the water, naked, or, as the not-thin Mary put it, "clothed only in her own fat."

By a singular, and not entirely happy coincidence, Mary had met a short time before (at Easter, 1906) a young Oxford student, who would soon decide to turn himself into an architect. His name was Geoffrey Scott, and Mary quickly fell deeply, chastely, but disastrously and possessively in love with him. Not long afterwards, through some English friends, the Houghtons, she met another budding architect named Pinsent, fortunately possessed of a more solid technical training. "A nice young architect named Cecil Pinsent came to call, and I found him here when I came in" — Mary's diary records on 12 January 1907 — "He is good-looking and seems *good*, as if he had been brought up by nice people. BB said he was intelligent too." Soon Pinsent was being shown around museums by Mary ("Pinsent . . . was terrifyingly appreciative of all I said . . . He did not . . . make a single banale remark, or admire anything wrong.")

That summer, while in England, Mary noted on 13 August 1907 "Took Scott to lunch with Cecil to discuss architectural possibilities. Cecil (being

Mary's loggia, at the southwestern corner of the house. Photo: David Morowitz

The west facade, with a wrought-iron door to the kitchen area, designed by Pinsent. The little loggia on the second floor, at right, opens off of what was Mary Berenson's room, now the bedroom of the Director. Photo: David Finn

just engaged) [to Alice Houghton, daughter of his patrons; the engagement was short-lived] treated it all very lightly, as if one's profession were a very irrelevant, secondary sort of matter: and Geoffrey's one idea was to find out how many holidays there were!" Mary should have been warned by Geoffrey's hostile attitude towards work, but when she was caught in the grip of one of her crushes, she was blind to any failing.

In introducing Scott to Pinsent, Mary wanted to help her beloved youth find some direction in his life. The introduction sowed a seed, but a very slow-growing one. The following fall Scott began studying, listlessly, at the Tufton Street School of Architecture (where Pinsent had studied earlier, with greater profit), writing at the same time to her that he felt "no latent capacity for drains and ventilators" As it happened, drains were going to prove one of I Tatti's most vexed problems; fortunately Pinsent actually enjoyed dealing with them.

Work on I Tatti could not begin immediately after its purchase, partly because of scarcity of funds and, more, because of Bernhard's commitment to complete the last of his surveys of Italian Renaissance painting, the *North Italian Painters*. A slow and tormented writer, Berenson struggled to finish the little book during the last months of 1906. And it was not until February 1907 that he could write the final words of the Preface. He then had to complete a taxing revision of the lists of paintings in all four volumes for an important reissue. Such revisions and amplifications were to remain a continuing occupation for the rest of his life.

At the beginning of 1908 Berenson allowed himself a pleasure trip to Rome, where he met some of his female admirers—the elegant Spanish-born Florentine Contessa Serristori and the bewitching, lively young American Gladys Deacon, later to become Duchess of Marlborough. That spring he and Mary joined their friend Carlo Placci and his nephews for a motor tour of Sicily, then a restful stay at the luxurious Villa Floridiana in Naples, occupied by friends of Placci's, before returning to I Tatti and—finally—to the real problems of rebuilding the house in a way that would satisfy the expanding demands of their increasingly sumptuous way of life.

They had little time, for they were off on an American tour in the autumn. In their inexperience and in their haste, they explained their architectural requirements to a local builder named Zannoni and to the foreman of the squad of workers, a man with the appropriately artistic name of Ammanati. Then the Berensons went off to London and the United States, leaving the job to be done—and supervised—by the two men who, as it turned out, did not get along.

The Berensons returned to London in the last week of March, 1909, after their satisfying and profitable American stay. A week later, Mary rushed off to Florence, while Bernhard set out on an extended Portuguese holiday with a party of rich friends, after which he would spend some time in Paris, while Mary dealt single-handed with the many problems at I Tatti.

GATEWAY IN THE OUTSIDE
WALL SEEN FROM THE CYPRESSES.

The terra-cotta vase
you bought

Wall
lavat

DOORWAY SEEN FROM THE ROUND
COUTYARD

Of the Ferrarese painter Ercole de' Roberti (ca. 1456-1496) Berenson wrote ". . . if you stop to think of the substance in the figures represented, you must conclude that they consist of nothing solid, but of some subtle material out of which they were beaten, like repoussé work, having no backs at all, or with hollow insides." But, in the same study, he also said: ". . . in his best pictures [. . .] the figures are so sharply silhouetted, and so frankly treated like repoussé work, that, far from taking them amiss, one is bewitched by their singularity." This Baptist, and a companion panel of St. Jerome, were acquired from the Aldo Noseda collection in Milan. Roberto Longhi attributed the two panels to Baldassare d'Este. Photo: David Morowitz

Of the Veneto painter Gian Battista Cima da Conegliano (ca. 1460–ca. 1518) Berenson wrote "no other master of that time paints so well the pearly hazes that model the Italian landscape with a peculiar lightness and breath [. . .] He is a draughtsman of strenuous and exquisite precision." This St. Sebastian—details of its acquisition are unknown—hangs in an upstairs corridor at I Tatti. Photo: David Finn

She and Bernhard exchanged almost daily letters, some of them unusually long. Arriving in Settignano, Mary found "the construction is done, and splendidly done, not a trace of shoddy work. The decoration is all to do. I see my way very well, and in the end we shall have, I think, a house that entirely suits us." This recklessly optimistic letter, dated 4 April, was followed by others, written in tones of increasing disillusion, amounting at times to despair. That first letter—written from Aunt Janet's villa, where Mary was staying temporarily—continued, already hinting at problems: "they won't give us electricity. We have the contract, and could enforce it by law [. . .] Ammanati doesn't advise this. [. . .] Ammanati [. . .] is a real brick. The delay is not his fault, it is ours for not giving him full authority over Zannoni, who has rather neglected us [. . .] It has rained steadily, for two months, hence the walls aren't dry, and the spots of new mortar, when fireplaces have been put in are damp."

"The new library is *glorious* but Houghton's furniture is a disaster."

This Javanese volcanic stone Buddha head was bought in Paris. According to Laurance Roberts, it probably came from Borobudur, the largest and most holy of the Buddhist temples of central Java. It is thought to date from the eighth century. Photo: David Finn

Geoffrey Scott, who—to Bernhard's irritation—was in Settignano with Mary, was "very ill and I've put him under a doctor's care." Geoffrey's frequent illnesses were to be another persistent theme in Mary's correspondence with Bernhard, arousing scant sympathy in the recipient, himself a slave to various recurrent complaints, largely gastric.

In another letter, apparently written the same day, Mary went into details: the *contadino's* house was too near the villa, the front terrace and the courtyard were filled with rubbish, the little wooden door to the library looked too *meschino* [wretched] and Mary would seek out a stone lintel . . . the iron balustrade bought for the stairway would not fit . . . part of the paint on the ceiling upstairs was dropping to bits . . . the three servants' rooms were damp and would not be habitable until autumn, there was no floor in the kitchen.

On the positive side: "the draining is all completely seen to [. . .] So thee [Mary addressed Berenson in the Quaker fashion] sees the *main things* (except the electricity) are done. And I truly think they *couldn't* have gone much further without me. I have hundreds of things to decide on [. . .] The details of the landscape gardening must wait for Logan [. . .]"

The letter goes on for another eight closely-written pages, ending with gossipy accounts of friends and visitors: Scott, Aunt Janet, the Hapgoods,

Mrs. Jephson, Horatio Brown, John Addington Symonds's crusty daughter, and Mary's former housekeeper Maud Cruttwell. To cap things, it was actually snowing: "I am glad thee isn't here."

The next day, another letter announced that the "kitchen floor was already half laid at ten o'clock." To spare Janet Ross trouble, Mary and Scott were moving to the nearby pension, the Villa Linda. Mary had hired a coach and coachman temporarily and there was a new cook at I Tatti, whose dinner, on 7 April, was "*discreto*, but I ate it alone and that is too severe a test."

Berenson was supposed to join her presently, but as the days passed, Mary became increasingly alarmed at the prospect of his arriving to find the villa in a state of confusion. His rages—frequently provoked by Mary's nonchalant domestic management—were terrible to behold; understandably, Mary, faced daily with countless decisions, was in consequence equally afraid of doing something wrong and bringing down upon herself still more tremendous reproaches. The wondrous serenity, the monastic quiet that guests, even then and still today, found in I Tatti were often achieved only at the price of volcanic fury and bitter pain. Soon the letters were largely devoted to preparing Bernhard for the confusion awaiting him.

Installed now in the Villa Linda, where Geoffrey was now staying, on 13 April, Mary wrote: "I hope to move into the villa in a fortnight, but there will be endless dust and confusion, and many workmen, and endless interruptions, for we will be at a moment when everything will be personally overlooked. *There is no other way* [. . .]" She then added a disarming PS: "I *love* doing this work for thee. I think of it a hundred times a day."

The following day, still from the pension: "I struggled over to the Villa, and was very glad I did so, as they were painting thy room an awful colour of green in the ceiling. It took nearly an hour to get the right colour—"

Scott continued to suffer ill health, so rather than a help, he constituted an added concern for Mary. Meanwhile her brother Logan had arrived. She consulted him about the question of Berenson's coming. On 15 April, she reports to Bernhard that, having sought Logan's verdict "about the state of fitness of the villa," her conclusion is that, on the whole, he should come, as there are some decisions that only he can make.

On 16 April, the new coachman was discovered selling stolen violets from the villa in town; he had also threatened the cook with violence "because he was given polenta to eat." Mary dismissed him.

Fortunately for Mary, Berenson had also made some mistakes, insisting on a wire fence around the property. Now installed, it made the place look "like a chicken run," as Mary bluntly pointed out.

Two days later, Mary casually mentions "the Houghtons want us to take Pinsent." And, again, on 20 April, she repeats: "[Mr. Houghton] strongly counseled our getting down Cecil Pinsent to play watch-dog. He said he would save us endless worries, and, in the end, expense. What does thee think? He could design our book-cases etc. at the same time [. . .]"

In the meanwhile Mary was seeking out all sorts of objects for the house, from practical things like stoves for the kitchen and door handles ("quite horrid and common, only they are comfortable to the hand and inoffensive, being white porcelain knobs. They had to go on before the doors were varnished") to the necessarily imposing stone doorway for the library and a wrought-iron gate for the entrance.

Much that was done had to be redone: "Thee wd. rage at seeing the way the red fire-place is put up—on a socle that doesn't even match it—but none was sent from Paris." This was the 23 April complaint; on the 24th she had worse news: "I can't get Pinsent, for Alice [Houghton, the daughter] is coming. They have just broken their engagement, and the Houghtons say they mustn't be here together."

Meanwhile, Mary was not only writing letters, but also receiving them, sometimes Bernhard's were "painful." But on 27 April, after the Houghtons had come up to lunch, she announced happily that "Pinsent *may* come after all."

Finally, at the end of the month, Berenson himself did come, lodging at Aunt Janet's where, Mary had assured him, he would be "well-valeted." After a deceptive few days of relative calm, he could control himself no more. As he wrote to his patroness, Isabella Stewart Gardner (in a letter chiefly devoted to a vain attempt to sell her a Manet): "I am nearly dead with disgust, rage, and despair over what has been done to our place. God knows whether it will ever again be beautiful, and whether I shall survive to see it." Calmer, he wrote again ten days later: "Trouble upon trouble in the house, but the weather is divine, Italy beautiful, and I do manage to enjoy a minute or two of the day."

By this time Pinsent had arrived and was put in charge, while the rejected Zannoni brought suit. The plumbing went to pieces; a burst boiler and a failed pump were followed by overflowing baths and newly-dampened walls. The telephone produced only unpleasant noises. Pinsent now shared Mary's terror of the master's frown.

When Berenson went off to Paris after a scant month at I Tatti, he left Pinsent in charge, but warned him severely about submitting and respecting estimates. Useless insistence: in his own way, Pinsent was as spendthrift as Mary in hers.

If these crises caused Mary much suffering, they had the beneficent effect of making her see the valetudinarian young Geoffrey Scott with new, slightly more opened eyes (assisted by the jaundiced view of Logan, as well). Mary urged Bernhard, in Paris, to help find Geoffrey a position; and when she left for Paris herself shortly after Bernhard's departure, Geoffrey went with her, to take up a job as assistant to the American architect and writer, Ogden Codman (Edith Wharton's collaborator on *The Decoration of Houses*). Geoffrey wrote a letter to Mary, grateful for having got him "anchored." But he was not out of her life or, even less, out of I Tatti.

Mary returned to I Tatti and its problems in September of 1909; Bernhard arrived on 30 October, to a triumphant welcome staged by Mary who,

Perhaps the prize of Berenson's Oriental collection, this gilt bronze altar of the Northern Wei dynasty (386–535) was also bought in Paris. It stands 62 cm. high, with its double pedestal. An inscription on the left side of the lower stand identifies the artist as Han Te-chou of Shuh Ai district, who made the image "for the Emperor, the people of the land, his contemporaries, his teachers, his father, his mother, his elder and younger brother, his sisters, and his relations."
Photo: I Tatti Archive

with their friend Robert ("Trevy") Trevelyan, had lined up the forty workmen and six servants for a ceremonial greeting. With Berenson came an eighth-century Buddha head he had purchased in Paris, the first important item in what was to be his small, but choice Oriental collection. Mary appreciated the head's "tactile values," but found it otherwise hideous. Mary's dislike of Oriental art did not keep Bernhard from forming a distinguished collection, but it may have discouraged him from enlarging that collection beyond a certain point.

Bernhard was hardly home before the French artist René Piot, whom he had met and liked in Paris the previous year, came to the house, bringing a scheme for frescoing the lunettes of the new library with illustrations of Virgil's *Georgics*. In an immediate burst of shared enthusiasm, Mary and Bernhard commissioned the decoration.

For the rest, the villa's defects immediately attracted Berenson's notice and provoked his contempt. Poor Pinsent was promptly blamed for the doors that

Berenson's engagement book during a stay in England reflects his social life. From a visit with Mary's daughter at Ford Place, Sussex, he motors back to London with Edith Wharton, stays with her and lunches with Lady Cunard, goes driving with Edith and Henry James, then lunches with James before returning to the country. Courtesy, I Tatti Archive. Photo: David Morowitz

would not shut or, if shut, would not open. Berenson fled first to Siena, then sought out the luxurious hospitality of the nearby Villa Gamberaia, Princess Ghyka's establishment. Fortunately, thanks largely to his association with the art dealer Joseph Duveen, he was now making an unparalleled amount of money. After buying first one, then a second motor car, he acquired a painting by the Venetian artist Cima da Conegliano for himself (probably the incomparable Saint Sebastian), and two "ruinously expensive" works by Luca Signorelli, portraits of the Vitelli brothers Camillo and Vitellozzo, which Berenson sent to the conservator Cavenaghi in Milan for restoration. They still hang today—where, on their arrival at I Tatti, Berenson put them—in the so-called "Signorelli corridor" linking his former study and bedroom with the library.

During another extended absence of Bernhard's, René Piot reappeared at the villa to execute his frescoes in the new library, pressing the reluctant Scott and Pinsent into service as his errand-boys (Mary soon put a stop to this). Neither Mary nor the two architects liked the frescoes, but—to their surprise—Berenson's initial reaction was not the violent disgust they had feared. As Mary wrote to her mother in that September of 1910: "[Piot] modified the vulgarity of the nudes and opened out a soft landscape behind."

The first four lunettes were finished in Bernhard's absence. Just before his scheduled return, Pinsent wrote in his notebook: "Unanimous decision to destroy Piot frescoes. But nothing is to be said. It is to take shape FIRST in B.B.'s mind."

On his return, in November, the decision took shape in his mind very quickly; the only question was what exactly to do with the offending work. Before announcing his intentions, he wrote a tactful letter to Piot to the effect that his eye, having been "formed on pictures faded and ruined by time," was not ready for the luxury of the frescoes. The tact was wasted: Piot was offended, but remained friends with Berenson, even after the frescoes were covered with blank canvas, matching the walls left unfrescoed. Over a decade after Berenson's death, under the direction of Craig Hugh Smyth, and at the request of a former Fellow, Carlo Del Bravo, the frescoes were uncovered as part of a city-wide exhibition of French paintings in Italian collections. They remain visible, as gaudy and inappropriate as they were at their creation, but a lasting, significant part of I Tatti's history.

It was not until a year later, after further absences, that Berenson was finally able sincerely to praise the work of his youthful architects. As Mary wrote, in September 1911 to her sister Alys (first wife of Bertrand Russell): "The new library is a dream [. . .] the frescoes gone [. . .] the house is as clean and dainty as a jewel." On 1 October, Bernhard arrived and, on seeing the library "clasped Cecil's hand in both his [. . .] and said it was the best he had done [. . .] surpassed anything he had hoped for [. . .] a dream of scholarly seclusion." Edith Wharton who, just at this time, came to I Tatti for the first of what was to become a series of annual visits for more than twenty years, wrote of her pleasure in Berenson's library: "I had never before stayed in a house where I could lead exactly the same life as in my own; working in the morning, and browsing at all hours in a library which, though incalculably bigger and more important than mine, was based on the same requirements; a broad and firm foundation of books of reference constantly replenished and kept up to date; all the still *living* classics, in Greek, Latin and and the principal modern languages, and an annual influx of the best in current letters [. . .] such a library as that of I Tatti is a book-worm's heaven; the fulfilment of all he has dreamed that a great working library ought to be [. . .] not a dusty mausoleum of dead authors but a glorious assemblage of eternally living ones."

Edith also had words of praise for the space itself: "This 'great good place,' which at first consisted of one noble room, lined with books to a high vaulted ceiling, and used not only as a library but as a living-room, was added to the original house by my dear friend Geoffrey Scott, and Cecil Pinsent, his partner; and they presently built out from it a wing containing two long conventual book-rooms with tall doors leading to a terrace of clipped box."

However scholarly the life of I Tatti then was, it was certainly not—despite Mary's description to Alys—completely secluded. The pattern of constant guests, for any or all of the daily three meals (tea was, and remains today, a social occasion, not a mere pause in the day's occupations), or

Overleaf:
The so-called "new" library, with the sixth-century A.D. (northern Qi dynasty) portrait of a Buddhist monk, known to the I Tatti staff affectionately as "the Chinese Madonna." Photo: David Morowitz

residents in the house's now functioning guest rooms, continued and waxed. Casual passers-through-Florence, perhaps with a letter of introduction, were invited to lunch or tea; closer friends and neighbors came for dinner. The guests who actually stayed in the house tended to be family, like Berenson's sisters or Logan or Mary's children or old regulars like Trevy.

In that autumn of 1911 Edith's initial visit sealed a valuable association. After a chilly first meeting some time previously, at Henry Cannon's villa La Doccia, the shy, often aloof novelist had become a friend of both Berensons, especially of Bernhard, who regularly visited her at one or another of her French houses. Like the Berensons, Mrs. Wharton adored motoring, and usually came with her chauffeur and her Mercedes, ready to whisk away her host and hostess on an excursion to some natural or artistic beauty otherwise hard to reach.

As Edith was the co-author of a book on interior decoration and the future author of a book on Italian gardens, the prospect of her first stay must have been daunting. She was lodged in what was called the "Ritz" suite (later it was sometimes referred to as 'Edith's rooms,' and Berenson's collection of her works is largely shelved in the sitting room-study).

Work on the actual house now slowed down, and Berenson could write to Henry Adams that "Mary had succeeded at last in knocking [the house] into shape," indeed, for a while building virtually ceased, but work on the garden was to continue for many years. In a sense, it has never stopped, as gardens invite—and require—constant intervention.

For the house, Bernhard had determined the grand lines, the general character of the construction; but for the garden, Mary took the lead. As Scott's biographer Richard Dunn says, after she engaged Pinsent—to be assisted by Geoffrey Scott—"in her typical way, Mary urged them to begin their work without consulting B.B."

But then, during one of Mary's absences in England, Bernhard discovered their plans by accident and, after Scott had walked around the grounds with him, describing their ideas, Berenson found them "promising," as he wrote to the absent Mary (February, 1911).

A month later Cecil wrote to Mary about progress on the two pools, the rustic wall, and the allée leading down from the steps "genuinely successful now that it has been tidied . . . and makes one feel the garden will not be a failure after all." Work proceeded during the following year; in June, Cecil and Geoffrey were setting out some topiary along the steps, and arranging a water garden and grotto in the lower gardens. The Firm (also called the Infirm, a joking reference to Scott's frequent illnesses) finally had received another important commission, the creation of the Villa Le Balze and its gardens for Berenson's Harvard contemporary the philosopher Charles Augustus Strong; but Pinsent and Scott continued to concern themselves with I Tatti, especially the grounds, now including a vegetable garden and the hay-shed [the future Granaio] in the servants' courtyard. Things still could go wrong, but the "boys," as they were called, dealt with most of the difficulties,

The second-floor corridor, just outside the Director's office. Photo: David Finn

as Mary wrote her family: "Geoffrey bears the brunt of them and B.B. knows nothing and I very little and humorously. How very different from the days when Cecil [. . .] muddled everything and B. B. cursed and I wrung my hands." By spring of 1913, this phase of work on the house, the library and the garden at I Tatti seemed to be finished; the architects could direct their attention elsewhere, and the Berensons also could think about other matters. Bernhard was deeply entangled in the most impassioned and troubling love-affair of his life, with the exotic Belle da Costa Greene, J. P. Morgan's assistant, while Mary was still unable to repress or temper her unrequited love for the elusive, ambiguous Geoffrey.

Fortunately, the economic side of their life was less tormented. One American collector and friend had given Bernhard some profitable stock market tips; and while he continued to work with other dealers, his association with the Duveens was by now flourishing and would be his mainstay for many years. Though he complained frequently about the commercializing of his knowledge, the Duveen connection would have made him financially, if not temperamentally, secure if he, in his way, had not been as extravagant as the over-generous Mary.

After a ritual Easter celebration in the I Tatti chapel, at which all the staff was present, Mary—writing to her mother—commented that it was "rather

Another view of the "new" library, designed by Pinsent and Scott in 1915 as an extension of the "main" library of the first version of the Berenson villa. Pinsent designed the wooden urns, which correspond to the stone urns in the *giardino pensile* (the walled "hanging" garden, beyond the door). Photo: David Morowitz

awful to think how many people live off B.B.'s interest in Italian art [. . .] seven servants, six contadini [peasants, or tenant farmers], two masons, one book-keeper, one estate manager, and their wives and children and then me, with a mental trail behind me of all the things I do and the people who look to me. And then B. B.'s whole family. Really it is a lot for the shoulders of one poor delicate man."

Berenson's thorough biographer Ernest Samuels gives a glimpse of I Tatti's intellectual life in these prewar years. At one dinner, the young John May-

nard Keynes argued about economics, trade, and taxation with Henry Cannon, the banker. The next day the Egyptologist and collector Theodore Davis seemed to Mary "a complicated and exhausting bore," and that same afternoon the Laboucheres' house-party—"riffraff" Mary called them—came to visit. But then the appearance of the young German philosopher Count Hermann Keyserling brought Berenson three days of "uninterrupted talk" and raised the tone of the villa's life along with his own spirits.

In mid-summer, before Mary made her regular visit to her family, and after Berenson had set off on his part-social, part-business, and part-scholarly travels, Mary had first to close up the house. Samuels describes this "formidable task": all the carpets had to be rolled up and carried off, a picture restorer mended any cracks in their panel paintings, woolen things were put away in camphor, a carpenter repaired furniture, frames might be regilded if necessary, mosquito netting was mounted, all mattresses were unstuffed and restuffed, books were carried off to be bound.

In the summer of 1911 three workmen were completing the so-called French salon, a little stuccoed chamber near the living room, while Geoffrey was measuring off the area of the next addition to the library. Four men were also required to "swathe" the library, prior to the stretching of the canvas false-walls to conceal the Piot frescoes (which Edith, in her memoirs, tactfully ignores).

Outside, as Pinsent later reported to Mary, a pebble pavement on the clipped box terrace was completed, and the stairs leading from the terrace to the lower garden were in place. In the fall, three hundred ilexes were ordered for the garden; they were forty feet tall, "so that Berenson could enjoy them in his lifetime." He was still enjoying them almost half-a-century later.

Bernhard was now beginning to find the villa habitable. And, most important, he was able to work there in always greater comfort. One of his fears was that, as he become increasingly embroiled in the business of expertise and sale, he would be able to write less, and thus his authoritative reputation—which

underpinned the value of his expertises—would dim. In the winter of 1913 he was "spinning out articles." That November, he and Mary made another successful trip to the States, leaving Geoffrey in charge of the house. An English couple named Gibson was occupying the Villino. The Berensons owned this capacious house across the road from I Tatti, and they sometimes used it for extra guests or lent it to friends for long periods. Scott dropped in on the Gibsons one day, and was introduced to an attractive young girl named Elisabetta Mariano, brought out to Settignano by her friend Byba Giuliani, also a friend of the Berensons.

Daughter of a Neapolitan intellectual and a Baltic noblewoman, cousin of an I Tatti visitor, the prickly philosopher Keyserling, Nicky—as Elisabetta was already called by everyone—had been brought up largely in Italy, in an unhappy household headed by an unsympathetic stepmother and an increasingly reclusive father. She had learned to think, and to see, for herself; and she described that crucial meeting in her *Forty Years with Berenson* (1966):

> [Scott] was looking after the decoration and furniture of various new rooms at I Tatti and at the same time was working on a book to be called *The Architecture of Humanism* [. . .] His voice, his laughter, his sense of fun, his whimsical expression, his choice of words all appealed to me. Physically, I found him rather unattractive and therefore considered him from the first moment not as a possible flirt but as somebody who might become a real friend [. . .] I was taken for the first time over the house and grounds of I Tatti.
>
> I was surprised to find the villa not a monumental one in the usual Florentine style with an imposing facade, but an unassuming, well-proportioned Tuscan house with a small enclosed lemon garden to the south and groups of old cypresses to both sides of it. Geoffrey's friend, the young English architect Cecil Pinsent, had used the underlying lemon house as a connecting link between the enclosed garden and the new formal one descending in terraces to an ilex wood. All this was in its infancy at the time of my first visit and looked out of proportion, the statues in the new formal garden ridiculously large as compared with the tiny box and cypress hedges. The long cypress avenue, the first addition made by the Berensons, was growing up well but looked puny against the majestic old cypresses near the house.

The interior made an even stronger impression on the bright young visitor: "[. . .] not so much for the size of the rooms as for the way in which they were furnished quietly, almost severely, with antique *credenze* and *cassoni*, comfortable chairs, Italian Renaissance paintings and sculpture mixed with Oriental sculpture and *objets d'art*. I had never seen anything like it before and it struck me as both fascinating and awe-inspiring."

Left:
Twin pools on the parterre of the formal garden. Photo: David Finn

Some time later, at the Scott-Pinsent apartment on Via delle Terme, in downtown Florence, Nicky went to a little party where she saw "a woman of majestic proportions and with fine regular features who at once came forward to greet me with a radiant smile [. . .]"

It was Mary. She promptly invited Nicky to lunch, perhaps having learned of Geoffrey's *coup de foudre* for the pretty young newcomer. The mistress of I Tatti then did everything possible to throw her protegé and Nicky together. The uninterested Nicky quickly saw through the scheme, and shortly thereafter went off on a trip to the Baltic, to visit relatives on her mother's side. Because of the first World War, Nicky did not return to Florence until the spring of 1919.

The outbreak of the war caught the Berensons in England, at Ford Place in Surrey, with Mary's family (her mother had died the previous year and the vast old family place, Friday's Hill, had been sold). No one, of course, had any idea how long the war would last; and both of Berenson's adopted countries—Italy and the United States—were neutral, but it was also uncertain how long that neutrality would last. At I Tatti, Cecil had provisionally interrupted work. Mary was inclined to sit out the war years—if years they proved to be—with her children in England; Bernard—as he was now styling himself—wanted to go to the States, and he insisted Mary should come with him.

It was a depressing time. The first war casualties were beginning to leave their mark: among the fallen was the Berensons' former manservant, young Henri, who had left I Tatti to go work for Edith in Paris, then had enlisted at the very outset of the war. Mary's son-in-law Adrian Stephen (brother of Virginia Woolf and husband of Karin) was a pacifist, as was Mary's former brother-in-law Bertrand Russell, now an outcast after separating from Alys. On a more practical plane, the art market seemed extinct; assets were frozen; Duveen was slow in paying a large outstanding debt. Mysteriously ill, Mary drew up a kind of letter-testament addressed to her daughter Ray: "If we die, thee and Oliver [Strachey, Lytton's brother and Ray's husband] and Karin had better go down with Adrian and arrange things. I think the photos and art library might be sold together and Messrs. Duveen would buy the pictures or some of them and perhaps Mr. Charles Freer of Detroit would buy some of the Chinese things . . . But" — Mary added, with her usual unsentimental realism—"I hope not to die now, when there is such a slump in works of art!"

England seemed narrow, provincial, so—as a first step—the Berensons went to Paris and spent ten days with Edith, whose waking hours were entirely taken up with her exhausting, time- (and money-) consuming war work. Then, as travel by train was banned, Mary and Bernard motored south, through France and northern Italy, to the uneasy peace of Settignano. They arrived in time for Christmas, 1914.

At last, Bernard was able to devote himself almost exclusively to writing, and that first wartime winter and spring were cheeringly productive. He began a series of six articles on "Venetian Paintings in the United States," which were published in the new and authoritative review *Art in America* over the rest of 1915 and in the first two numbers of 1916. Before 1916 ended, he had written two more articles on the same subject. All together, they formed the basis of a book published in 1916, when he also issued his *The Study and Criticism of Italian Art, third series*.

Though some of the foreign colony had left Italy and the stream of visitors from abroad had dwindled to the tiniest trickle, Bernard was not in want of company. Most afternoons, he called for the car and was driven over to the Villa Medici, where he visited the lovely, rich, and demanding Lady Sybil Cutting. Florentine gossips assumed they were lovers, and though still unsure whether they were or not, Mary became intensely jealous and developed a particular dislike for Lady Sybil, who then made matters much worse—and a great deal more complicated—by becoming engaged to young Geoffrey Scott, marrying him just before the war's end. The marriage was not a happy one for anybody, and it created a severe rift between Geoffrey and Mary, never truly healed, even after he was divorced from Lady Sybil. After producing a still-admired essay, *A Portrait of Zélide*, Scott was later commissioned to work on the newly-discovered Boswell papers. This position required him to live in America; sadly, as he had finally found an occupation which pleased him and at which he excelled (he proved a model editor), he died in New York in 1929, aged forty-five.

The history of a house (or its biography, as it might preferably be called in this case) is not just an account of its walls, its furnishings, its setting; nor is it simply a record of those who resided in the house, those who visited there, who fell in love there, who worked and died there. A house consists, to be sure, of its architecture and decoration, and also of its inhabitants. But its history should narrate the relations between the former and the latter.

In the case of I Tatti, the inhabitants' tales have often been told, sometimes well, sometimes less so. Berenson has been the subject of three biographies, of which Ernest Samuels's is by far the best, the most complete, the most impartial; Nicky Mariano's autobiography is as charming—and also as discreet—as she was in person. When Richard Dunn's biography of Geoffrey Scott is published, another bright patch of color will be added to the grand collage. And, as I Tatti welcomed many writers, the house and its people appear in countless memoirs and letters: from Edith Wharton and Logan Pearsall Smith and George Santayana in the earlier years, to Kenneth Clark and John Pope-Hennessy and Iris Origo (Lady Sybil's gifted daughter) in later days.

Each saw the house from a different angle, and—over the course of his long life—Berenson himself saw it differently, as he and the house changed and adjusted to each other more and more closely.

Through 1915 Mary and Bernard stayed mostly in Italy, at I Tatti, where

The formal garden seen from the Limonaia. At the end of the pebble-mosaic walk, the cropped ilex grove serves—in Pinsent's intention—as a defining base for the view of the city and hills to the south. Dominating the foreground of that distant view is the lovely little qattrocentro church of San Martino a Mensola, founded by Saint Andrew in the ninth century. Nicky and her sister, Baroness Alda Anrep, lived in the adjacent monastery after Berenson's death. It is now divided into five apartments where Fellows live. Photo: David Morowitz

both of them were frequently, admittedly bored. Finally, at the beginning of 1916, Mary managed to get to England to be with Karin, who was about to have a baby. When the child (a boy, Christopher) was born, Mary supervised domestic arrangements, hired a nanny and, once Karin was settled, joined Bernard in Paris. She disliked the social round there as much as he liked it, and was happy to leave the city with him, first for a trip to Spain, then for a visit to their friends the Curtises in the south. By January 1917 they were back at I Tatti.

After Italy's belated intervention on the side of the Allies, the male servants were called up, and the day-to-day running of the establishment became more and more difficult. Scott was in Rome, and Pinsent had joined the Red Cross. Pressed by the Duveens—for despite the war, the art market was becoming lively again—Berenson had to continue his dealing in what he contemptuously and self-laceratingly called the "pig trade."

As the war continued, and especially after the Americans came into it, Berenson chafed more and more at his Italian isolation. Visiting Paris to discuss Duveen business, he invoked Edith Wharton's aid, and with a bit of string-pulling, he finally was given an official position, as a consultant to U.S. military intelligence. Besides requiring him to reside in his beloved Paris, the job chiefly entailed hosting or attending frequent high-level lunches and reading foreign newspapers. He set himself up in an elegant apartment and led a busy social and cultural life, while performing his anything but onerous duties. He stayed on in Paris after the war's end to observe the peace talks and enjoy the company of the many highly-placed acquaintances who flocked to the French capital, which was beginning to resemble the Vienna of the 1815 Congress.

Mary, remaining at I Tatti, received from Paris instructions for making I Tatti proof against requisition (Florence was filling up with refugees from war-torn northern Italy who needed housing). Bernard's business correspondence—involving delicate negotiations with, among others, Mrs. Gardner, his chief client—was to be packed, with other sensitive documents, in a strong trunk, without his name on it, and stored with Lady Sybil at the Villa Medici. He also instructed Mary to send him his best summer underwear, some pyjamas, a morning coat, tails, and other items.

It was while Mary was preparing I Tatti for a long absence—planning to join Bernard then in Paris—that she received the shattering news of Geoffrey's engagement to her arch-rival Lady Sybil. Bernard was only mildly sympathetic with Mary's distress, as he regaled her with long accounts of his fascinating life in Paris, his encounters with Proust and Gide and old friends like the society decorator Elsie de Wolfe and the poet and literary hostess Nathalie Barney.

Mary remained at I Tatti until mid-February of 1918, often ill and lonely. Scott, who had a job at the British Embassy in Rome, tried to retain her friendship, despite his betrothal, but his letters only made matters worse. She begged to be allowed to come to Paris, but Berenson—not pleased by the prospect of dealing with her illness and unhappiness at close hand—kept putting her off. Finally, early in 1918, he consented. But Paris (where Bernard was embarking on another passionate affair) only worsened her condition. Her depression became suicidal, and her daughter Ray came to Paris to collect her and take her to a nursing home at Chobham, in England. An operation for "female ailments" led only to further ailments and an apparent breakdown. She was never to be really well after that.

In April of 1919, as Bernard stayed on in Paris, Mary returned briefly to I Tatti. She wrote to him after her arrival: "[. . .] I called on Mme Giuliani to get news of Nicky Mariani [sic] who just escaped, by the skin of her teeth, falling into the hands of the Bolsheviks who burnt down her brother-in-law's castle [. . .] Nicky is in Switzerland with Byba Giuliani, but they are expected here in a day or two. I want to see her, as I have my eye on her for a secretary-housekeeper. That is if she must earn money."

Meanwhile, as Nicky in Switzerland was waiting for her passport to be put in order, Mary was offering her, via phone calls to Byba, the job at I Tatti, secretly hoping that the attractive young girl would fall in love with Geoffrey, and then Mary would have both of them under her wing and eyes. But like so many of Mary's intrigues, this one went violently wrong. Geoffrey had fallen for Nicky, all right (who was indifferent to him), but in her wartime absence, he had now married Lady Sybil, for whom Mary nurtured a naked hatred.

But I Tatti was not forgotten. Earlier, Berenson had written from Paris to Mary, in England: "My heart begins to fail me. I think of my library, my leisure, my work, and have a fear of inchoating my holiday life with the aridity of a work-a-day one."

Berenson, however, had strong feelings about the war and, especially, about its aims. His contempt for the Italians' price for joining the allies (annexation of territory in the Tyrol and Dalmatia, dominion over the Adriatic and the Dodecanese) he found revolting, and his attitude towards the territorial ambitions of France and Britain was equally severe. He came to hate the unrelieved vindictiveness of the Allies against the Germans, as their defeat approached and anti-German virulence was more and more in evidence.

But the last furious fighting of the enemy in Italy, the disaster of Caporetto, which filled Florence with Friulian refugees, frightened him; he worried about the vulnerability of the unoccupied villa, which could be requisitioned. Mary was finally able to return there for a while, but left again in February of 1918 to remain away for a full year. Significantly, in June, when Bernard—a foreign-born citizen—had to renew his documents in Paris, he gave his legal residence as Boston, listing I Tatti as a "temporary local address."

In the spring of 1919, before the Berensons had returned to I Tatti,

Nicky Mariano was shown over the villa by the renegade Scott, who still had access to it. While Geoffrey looked at the library with the saddened eyes of memory, Nicky was inspecting it as her likely place of future employment: "[when] I had my first look around the library, what struck me was the vast number of unopened parcels of books that had arrived ever since 1917. Geoffrey seemed rather casual and aloof, praised the library as a wonderful place for browsing, pointed to a comfortable chair in the small library as the best place for undisturbed reading. I felt doubtful about ever having the leisure to occupy it." It may have been the chair in which Cyril Connolly on a later visit was to read Joyce's *Ulysses*.

Despite his marriage, and despite Nicky's reiterated lack of interest in him as an object of romance, Geoffrey continued his unwelcome courtship, with carefully calculated surprise meetings, long walks and talks, constant letters (delivered by hand to the Giuliani's villa where Mary was temporarily staying). Finally, the embarrassed Nicky had a little heart-to-heart with Lady Sybil, and there was a sharp tug on Geoffrey's leash.

The minor details of a long-ago romantic labyrinth would be of scant interest now were it not for the fact that, in the history of I Tatti, Nicky Mariano was to play a leading role. Meanwhile, a letter from the absent Mary had confirmed Nicky's appointment as librarian, assuring her that Berenson was not prejudiced against her because of her inexperience. The previous occupant of the post, Lance Cherry (killed at the front in 1915), had been a professional librarian, and Bernard had been more irritated by his professionalism than he would have been by amateurishness. So through the summer of 1919 Nicky unwrapped the parcels of books and put them in order. The quietness of the house was interrupted only once when during political upheavals in August a troop of rioters appeared at the gate and clamoured for wine. The butler who kept the keys of the cellar was off duty and, "enraged, [. . .] the rioters ended by forcing the door of the cellar[. . .]" They took away twenty-one bottles of whisky, two of cognac, three of champagne, ten of Rhine wine, and six flasks of oil.

This example of Italian unrest at the end of the war was a hint of the greater unrest to come, culminating in the establishment of the Fascist regime, which Berenson hated viscerally from its very outset. As the regime proceeded, Bernard's outspoken and well-known anti-Fascism led him to break with many Italian friends, and also provoked many arguments with British and American friends, who considered the Duce an Italian savior.

In Paris Berenson saw a good deal of the younger Sicilian writer and scholar Gaetano Salvemini, many of whose political ideas matched his own. Their friendship lasted through the ardent anti-Fascist Salvemini's exile—much of it spent at Harvard, where he inspired generations of students—and his return to Italy at Fascism's downfall.

Left:
The canopied ilex allée before trimming, with the cypress allée behind it.
Photo: David Finn

In September 1919, when Nicky had been installed for several months in the library, Mary returned, bringing with her from Paris a young American named Carl Hamilton, who had ingratiated himself with Bernard in Paris. Unlike most of her young enthusiasms, Carl was rich, and he seemed intelligently interested in collecting. He had hardly arrived at I Tatti before he extravagantly offered to buy all the Berenson pictures. After the offer was politely rejected, Mary, as a token of her affection—and apparently without consulting Bernard—gave their new friend a little painting of *St John in the Desert* (left to herself, she might well have sold him the collection). When Bernard found out, he was furious (even though Hamilton did become a friend and a good client for a while); and years later when, in economic distress, Hamilton sold the painting, now recognized as a valuable and rare Domenico Veneziano, for close to half a million dollars, Bernard's fury was revived and redoubled.

On arriving, Mary immediately welcomed Nicky into I Tatti's family, writing to Bernard that she was "completely *unsereiner* [a Berensonism meaning "our kind"]." And she went on: "the most congenial woman I have come across in years, perhaps ever. And such a lady!" Mary invited the somewhat bewildered neo-librarian to join her and Hamilton on a motor excursion. And, in Florence, the older woman took the young newcomer along on visits to neighbors and friends, including Janet Ross and Lina, and invited her

When distinguished visitors came to I Tatti, often a souvenir group photograph was taken (other photographs also recorded excursions from the villa). Here, in 1937, Nicky and Berenson are seen with Walter Lippmann. Carlo Placci, Berenson's long-time friend—until they quarreled over politics—stands between him and Lippmann. The figure at far left is Lucius Wilmerding, a friend of Lippmann's. Courtesy, I Tatti Archive. Photo: David Morowitz

The Villino, where many of Berenson's—and now the Center's—guests have stayed. Photo: David Finn

regularly to join the I Tatti table for her meals. The month after Mary's reappearance at the villa, it was Bernard's turn to make his rentrée. Nicky tells of the event in her memoirs: "I was not in the house when he arrived but was told by Mary next morning that he had immediately noticed the disappearance of the small painting . . ." Mary then referred to his "unreasonable and undignified rage." "Later that same morning while working at the end of the small library I heard a light step and saw B. B.'s slender elegant figure walking towards me. I was too flustered to say much, noticed his beautiful eyes and his charming smile, heard him utter a few words of appreciation of what I was trying to do and then he was gone."

The stream of guests began to flow again, and the first to turn up was the French writer Abel Bonnard, whom the Berensons took on an Umbrian motor tour, inviting Nicky along. In the spring of 1920, with the visit of Belle Greene, Bernard's former passion, Nicky had her first opportunity to act as buffer and intermediary on the occasion of one of Bernard's rages and Mary's subsequent fit of despair. Her value as peace-maker was quickly recognized, and her gentle serenity gradually came to give the house a new atmosphere, more conducive to work and relaxation. Perhaps inevitably, the thirty-two-year-old Nicky fell in love with Bernard, who fell in love with her. Fortunately, Mary—also totally under Nicky's spell—gave the reciprocated devotion her tacit blessing. As her health worsened until she became practically an invalid, Berenson's rages vanished. Despite his deep attachment to Nicky, his infatuations with handsome women did not entirely cease, and Nicky on more than one occasion had to bite the bullet. Berenson's appreciation of physical beauty never abandoned him, and attractive female visitors to I Tatti, even when its master was in his nineties, were

suprised, amused, and also flattered to feel the tactile hand on their knee beneath the table-cloth.

As Fascism began to tighten its grip not only on Italian government but also on Italian culture and thought, Berenson's unwavering opposition to the regime and his contempt of its supporters (which included many Italian intellectuals and also a number of highly-placed Americans) did not go unnoticed. When Salvemini, required to flee the country secretly, stayed at I Tatti before his departure—during the Berensons' absence—and then took refuge in England with Mary's brother and sister, Berenson was considered no better than a spy. Italian friends, even anti-Fascist ones, were more careful about visiting him; and when Walter Lippman wrote, planning a visit, Bernard had to warn him off, as such a visit could have unpleasant consequences for both of them.

The looming threat of expulsion from Italy, with consequent separation from his library, his garden, and Italian beauty, caused Berenson to curb his tongue a bit in public and to moderate his tone also in his letters and over the telephone, both of which could easily be monitored.

Still, for most of the 1920's, he could continue to travel, making visits to his friend the Crown Prince in Sweden, and, of course, to Edith at her various French establishments. Sight-seeing in Egypt, Sicily, Palestine, Spain, and in Italy itself entailed long absences from the villa. Since Nicky now regularly accompanied him and, health permitting, so did Mary, I Tatti was sometimes left in the care of the servants or of Nicky's sister Alda baroness Anrep and her husband, who for years were Berenson's guests at the Villino. On at least one occasion, a recent and highly-prized friend Harry Coster (married to Nicky's friend Byba), acting American consul, moved into the villa for its greater safety.

Even Mussolini could not stop Mary's *furor aedificandi*. In the fall of 1924, while the Berensons and Nicky were taking a working holiday in Rome, Mary decided to surprise Bernard with some improvements carried out in their absence: a fireplace in his bedroom, a relocation of the servants' hall and the wine cellar, and—most prominent—a clock tower to crown the south facade, on the axis of the main steps from the terrace, through the Limonaia to the lower formal garden. Designed by Pinsent before he had left the area, the tower would be constructed by a Florentine. As so often in the case of I Tatti's improvements, this job was delayed. But in the spring of 1926, when the travelers returned from an exciting tour of Sicily, the "surprise" was in place. Originally the tower was to have included a glassed-in room for Mary's sunbathing (a feature that would certainly have affected the serenity of the garden below); and the clock would, she thought, "lead the eye up and end the line of the garden path."

Even in its more modest proportions, the clock—with its blue face and silver hands—was something, indeed, of an eye-catcher. Berenson's first reaction was a mere grunt, as he seemed hardly to notice it. But then, on

another return, the following spring, he inspected the garden and the tower more carefully and shouted wrathfully: "You simply don't care how I feel. Your one idea is to give that insolent, unbearable Cecil something to do." The tower had to be made still smaller, but it remained and now seems a natural, attractive element of the house's structure.

In her reminiscences of life at I Tatti with Berenson, Nicky Mariano refers to the period between 1931 and 1938 as the "Janus-faced years." In fact, the life of the villa was somehow schizophrenic. There were the problems of

View southward from Berenson's study, now the Director's sitting room. Photo: David Morowitz

The east façade of the villa, with the arches designed by Pinsent (leading to the kitchen courtyard) and the corridor above connecting the oldest part of the house with the first Berenson additions.
Photo: David Morowitz

political tension (as Fascism flourished in Italy, the even more frightening prospect of Nazism was increasingly present in Germany) and the state of Mary's health. After another operation in the autumn of 1931, she became practically an invalid, often confined to her room or, at best, to the house and its grounds.

The other face of I Tatti was represented by the steady work on the revision of Berenson's epoch-making book on Florentine drawings, lightened

The enclosed garden in spring.
Photo: I Tatti Archive

by the arrival of new friends and old, and interrupted by occasional trips.

Already a decade earlier, Berenson had invited the first of what was to prove a series of younger aspiring scholars to come and live in the Villino and work with him on some of the more tedious aspects of the revisions, first of the famous lists of paintings, then on the drawings. Kenneth [later Lord] Clark had been the initial, and not entirely satisfactory, disciple. Though Clark felt profound respect for Berenson, who quickly appreciated the keen eye, the vast culture, and the lively ability of the young assistant, the relationship—after a promising start—did not prosper. It failed partly because, though he had not informed Berenson, Clark was engaged to be married before he took up residence at I Tatti, and though his attractive wife Jane charmed the I Tatti family, she was, in Berenson's eyes, a distraction; and moreover, Clark's undisguised ambition was not such as to allow him to spend day after day puzzling over some small detail of the work of a minor artist—the very details that so fascinated Berenson and made—and still make—the lists irreplaceable to amateurs and scholars.

Though she never claimed to be an art historian or any kind of expert, Nicky herself was able to give Berenson considerable help, especially on the Florentine drawings, which she found more congenial than the lists.

A few years after Kenneth Clark's departure, a charming Harvard graduate, John Walker, turned up in Florence and eventually moved into the Villino. Then, in the 'thirties, the young Benedict Nicolson (son of Harold Nicolson and of Vita Sackville-West), asked to be allowed to work under Berenson, and though he did not then become an official B.B. "assistant," he entered I Tatti's circle and became a frequent and welcome guest. The series continued with John (later Sir John) Pope-Hennessy, who first visited I Tatti—for tea with Mary— in the summer of 1936, becoming later a friend of Bernard's, as well as an informative correspondent, and disciple. For Pope-Hennessy, too, the villa had a Janus-faced character: "I did not then [1936] realize that I Tatti, as structure and idea, was a theme that would recur through my whole life. When I first went there I knew the outside of the villa from photographs of the two great *Olea fragrans* flanking the path down to the *limonaia* and the terraced garden sloping down the hill. But I found the inside, despite the presence of great works of art, a little daunting. There, in the downstairs room in which I first met Berenson, was the great *St. Francis in Ecstasy* of Sassetta with its two accompanying saints and a miraculous *Madonna* of Bernardo Daddi. It was midsummer, so daylight was excluded, and by dim electric light they looked like visions of works of art rather than originals. The upstairs corridor was lined with pictures, the Giotto *Entombment* and the Signorelli portraits of the Vitelli and small panels, some of which, to my embarrassment, I could not identify. In the library [. . .] I looked with alarm at the long wooden table at which I should eventually find myself studying photographs and the deep leather armchairs . . . The most unnerving feature of the house in those days was its quietness. It was a temple where the prevailing silence was never, save at mealtimes, broken by a human voice."

An early photograph of I Tatti showing the gardens before their definition. The cypress allée (puny, as it appeared to Nicky on first acquaintance) can be seen at left, descending from the house. The formal gardens do not yet exist, nor does Mary's clock-tower. The penciled rectangle indicated how the Berensons wanted the picture cropped to make a postcard for guests. Poggio Gherardo is visible at far left, beyond the sparse vegetation of the then virtually undeveloped countryside. Courtesy, I Tatti Archive. Photo: David Morowitz

It should be noted that this silence—which, in the library proper still reigns today—was thoroughly broken once the working day was over. Though voices were rarely raised, there was a great deal of talk. And the history of I Tatti is, to a large extent, also the history of the people who came there to talk and listen to Berenson. Some were famous, or became famous—the composer Roger Sessions, the Aldous Huxleys, Judge Learned Hand, Lowes Dickinson—others were bright, younger friends who were admitted to the circle of the elect, the "*unsereiner.*" Among the most appreciated members of this group was Count Umberto Morra, who had first come to I Tatti as a young man, in 1925, to deliver a message from his friend Salvemini, a message that, in those days of the regime, could not be conveyed by post or telephone. Morra, a polyglot cosmopolite and liberal intellectual, came from a family with close connections to the House of Savoy and thus impervious to Fascist suspicion. He remained until Berenson's death a helpful and valued friend, often a traveling companion and interlocutor.

Entranced by Berenson's conversation, for a period in the 'thirties he tran-
scribed as many of Berenson's words as he could remember into notebooks,
in his bedroom before retiring. Berenson was unaware of the presence of this
Boswell; the "conversations," published in 1965, give only a partial idea of
what it was like to converse with Berenson, since Morra does not include
anything said by the other participants in the lively talk. Thus the master of
I Tatti sounds like a monologuist, given to uttering *obiter dicta*, whereas he
was—and this is admittedly impossible to convey—also frequently silent;
and his speech was prompted and intertwined with the speech of others.

Through Morra, the young writer Alberto Moravia, still in his twenties
was also introduced into the circle. Moravia has also left valuable recollections of I Tatti in the 'thirties, and used Berenson as a much-distorted model
for a character in his late novel *1934.*

The complexion of I Tatti's troupe was subtly changing: there were fewer
members of the ingrown Anglo-Florentine set, fewer Maud Cruttwells and
Miss Bloods, but—on the one hand—more scholars and political thinkers,
while—on the other hand—there were just as many countesses and perhaps
more royals.

The paintings in the Berenson
collection have as a rule not been
cleaned. A rare exception is this
panel depicting *The Dying Virgin
Taking Leave of the Apostles* by the
Master of the Osservanza
Triptych. Originally attributed,
by Berenson and others, to
Sassetta, the panel is now
generally considered the work of
an artist in the group around
Sassetta. Berenson at one time
identified the painter as Sano di
Pietro, a view shared by Cesare
Brandi and John Pope-Hennessy.
Photo: David Morowitz

Opposite:
Bergognone, *Madonna and Child*, detail.
Photo: David Morowitz

4

*A*s the 1930's approached their end, Berenson became increasingly concerned with the political sufferings of Europe, and he became more intensely aware of his own ethnic background. He had long had complex feelings about being Jewish, and at times his critical attitude seemed almost to approach anti-Semitism. But he had always had Jewish friends—the American writer Israel Zangwill, for one, and Salomon Reinach, in Paris, for another—and as he saw friends and acquaintances in Germany, then in Austria, then in Italy, losing their jobs, their nationalities, even their lives, he devoted more of his thought and his support to others in their plight.

His own plight was, to be sure, cause for concern. Long before the infamous Italian "racial laws" of 1938, prohibiting Jews from attending university, teaching, performing military service, among other restrictive indignities, Berenson had been under the watchful eye of the police simply for being a foreigner and an avowed opponent of the regime. His Jewishness only made worse an already bad situation. He left I Tatti less and less often, and the visitors' list grew shorter. He heard, with alarm, the news of friends and acquaintances like Bruno Walter, hounded from his position and his country.

And, closer to home, as Nicky Mariano recounts, a wealthy Italian Jew who came to I Tatti to discuss the situation, told Berenson that, even in his own home, he did not feel safe; Berenson questioned his next visitor, his doctor, about this assertion; the doctor repeated the conversation, and it reached the ears of the police, who summoned Nicky to the police station. Though she resolutely denied everything, the Jewish visitor was arrested and eventually confined on the Tremiti islands.

In August of 1939, meeting Berenson and Nicky at an exhibition in Geneva, Prince Paul of Yugoslavia urged Bernard not to return to Italy. Ignoring this advice, he went back to I Tatti anyway, and two weeks later the Nazi-Soviet pact was announced. Nicky and Berenson continued to travel, mostly inside Italy, and they were in Rome in June 1940, when Italy declared war on the Allies.

Berenson's instinct was to return at once to I Tatti, but Countess Serristori sent him word to stay put, as hostile rumors were circulating in Florence, identifying him as a dangerous spy. Part of the problem was Mary, who insisted on filling the house with people—largely foreigners—and giving unsuitably late parties.

I Tatti was finally emptied of foreign visitors, and of foreign servants (the chauffeur Parry and the maid Elizabeth took the last train for England on 10 June, were stopped in France and arrested by the Germans). The Berensons' combative Swedish masseuse Naima Loforth was also arrested, and

Harold Acton's elderly parents were briefly jailed before being allowed to leave for Switzerland.

The Berensons, during these fraught months, were recipients of considerable, and conflicting advice. American friends, Gordon and Elizabeth Morrill, cabled from America to "stay put," and William Phillips, the American ambassador and former admirer of the Duce, took Nicky into the garden of the ambassadorial residence in Rome in May of 1941, to say, safely out of earshot: "My advice would be for B.B. to stay on in Florence and not to try to go away. His property is very valuable and his personal presence would be the best protection for it."

It was the same ambassador who, a few weeks later, intervened to have an expulsion order for Berenson canceled, when warned by Nicky of its having been issued. Mary, on being told of the arrival of British officers, prisoners to be confined in Temple Leader's Vincigliata castle up the road, characteristically exclaimed; "What fun it will be to have them drop in for tea."

Through all this, a few Italian scholars continued to come to the library to pursue their research, and the braver of them occasionally slipped into the sitting room at tea-time for some Berenson conversation. The villa's telephone was cut off—to prevent the "spy" Berenson from communicating with other agents, presumably—but after protests, a telephone was installed, not in the villa, but in the house of the young and resourceful estate manager, Geremia Gioffredi.

Still, communication with the outside world became more and more problematical. The foreign newspapers, on which Bernard was dependent, failed to arrive. When the *Züricher Zeitung* stopped coming, I Tatti had to recur to the Nazi-controlled *Deutsche Allgemeine*, which Berenson found full of interesting information, between the lines. The post was irregular, and the radio totally unreliable.

Valuable information arrived indirectly. From Rome, Umberto Morra collected embassy gossip and transmitted it in prudent circumlocution; the sudden and frequent appearance in his letters of a mysterious friend named "Edward" might today puzzle an unprepared reader, but it soon becomes clear that "Edward" stands for "England," and his decisions and indecisions reflect those of Chamberlain and Hoare. Finally, when the Allies landed in Sicily, Alda Anrep's milk boy delivered the news along with the milk, and Alda transmitted it to I Tatti.

Two weeks after the milk boy's report of the Allied landing in Sicily, the I Tatti community learned of the fall of Mussolini, in the night between 24 and 25 July. The dictator's arrest and imprisonment was the spark that lighted bonfires of joy in Italian cities, as the same crowds that had cheered his histrionic public appearances now celebrated his defeat, after he had brought defeat to the nation.

A day or so later, a great friend of Berenson's and Nicky's, Carlotta Orlando (daughter of Vittorio Orlando, prime minister of Italy at the time of the Paris conference) walked the twenty-five kilometers from Vallombrosa to Settignano to see how her friends were getting along, and to warn them—as did other Italian friends—that "if the Germans should be in full control of Italy and this time not as allies but as enemies he [Berenson] cannot go on staying at I Tatti. As an American, as a well-known anti-Fascist, as a Jew, he is in immediate danger . . ."

They did not have long to wait. On 8 September 1943, when the Allies prematurely announced the signing of an armistice with the Italian govern-

ment headed by General Badoglio, German forces promptly assumed control of as much of Italy as was not already occupied by the Allies. The king and the royal family and the government hastily abandoned Rome, the Italian army disintegrated, and the roads north were occupied by deserting soldiers trying to get home. News reports were contradictory and unhelpful, yet all-important decisions had to be made, and made quickly.

At I Tatti there were the Berensons, Nicky, and the remaining servants; the Anreps were away at Montecatini for the waters. Nicky took the bus into Florence and, walking past German forces, consulted their friend the Marchese Filippo Serlupi, who—among other things—was officially the ambassador of the Republic of San Marino to the Holy See. Thus Le Fontanelle, his villa above Careggi, to the north of Florence, enjoyed diplomatic immunity. He invited Bernard and Nicky to take refuge there.

Once back at I Tatti, Nicky managed to despatch a car to Montecatini for her family, asking them to move into the house during what everyone thought would be a brief absence (the Allies seemed to be proceeding rapidly northward from Sicily and Salerno).

The departure was abrupt, as Nicky later wrote: "We left without telling Mary where we were going. Her natural optimism and her contempt for any kind of prudence or secrecy made her incapable of even imagining any real danger."

Saint Benedict Receiving a Young Monk, a small (16 x 33 cm.) panel by the fourteenth-century Florentine artist Nardo di Cione. It is the predella of a large painting of the saint now in the National Museum, Stockholm. As with so many works in Berenson's collection, the date of acquisition and the provenance are unknown. Photo: David Morowitz

The Serlupi villa is not within easy walking distance of I Tatti, but it was soon possible to establish sporadic communication. Cecil Anrep, Nicky's nephew, was sometimes able to bring messages, and Nicky herself was able to steal brief moments at I Tatti, when Berenson could be left alone. When they were barely settled in the villa, Nicky received a message (via Cecil Anrep) from the German consul, asking her to come and see him. Though she had never met him, she knew he was a confirmed anti-Nazi, and she went to the consulate in Via de' Bardi in good spirits. "I was received at once

When Berenson bought this panel, through Trotti et Cie., Paris, in 1911, it was thought to be by Benvenuto di Giovanni, but the new owner soon attributed it to the Sienese Girolamo di Benvenuto (1470–1524). In the catalogue of the Berenson Collection, published by Ricordi after Berenson's death, the work is entitled "Madonna appearing to Patrician John and His Wife." Berenson's friend and colleague Mason Perkins thought the subject was a miracle of Saint Nicholas. Later both Perkins and Berenson agreed that it represents the Appearance of the Virgin to Beato Lucchese and His Wife. The work is part of the predella of a large altarpiece in the Siena Pinacoteca; other parts of the predella have been identified in various private collections, including a *Miracle of the Snows*, which belonged to Berenson's one-time disciple and long-time enemy, the late Roberto Longhi, in Florence. Photo: David Morowitz

and found that the consul's face and expression corresponded to what I had heard about him. Both inspired me with the greatest confidence."

After some nervous small-talk, the consul finally "came out with the assurance that he would do all within his power to protect the collection and library of I Tatti." Herr Wolff then added that it would be easier for him to carry out his good intentions if Berenson was no longer in the house. When Nicky told him that Berenson was already elsewhere, the kindly diplomat seemed greatly relieved. Nicky later commented, in her memoirs: "This eased my conscience as it proved [. . .] the decision to take B. B. away had been the right one."

On good days, Berenson would try to take his afternoon walk; and at least one neighbor, a young student (now a successful New York lawyer) who also liked walking, recalls meeting—and recognizing—Berenson in the woods above Montughi. Seeking to spare the Serlupis any extra burdens, Berenson sent his linen—including his easily-identified monogrammed shirts—over to I Tatti by bicycle to be laundered, even when there were Germans in the villa.

At first, thinking to be away from I Tatti only for a matter of a few weeks, neither Berenson nor Nicky had taken provisions for a long stay. Their hosts somehow managed to feed them—and an assortment of other "guests," ranging from members of the Italian royal family to Jewish refugees. But it was hard for Berenson to work, so he exercised his mind by reading, voraciously and unsystematically, and by keeping a diary. The results of those activities were two of his most charming and widely-read works: *One Year's Reading for Fun* and the diaries entitled *Rumor and Reflection*, the intellectual fruit of what turned out to be almost thirteen months of exile.

Life at I Tatti, during the absence of Berenson and Nicky, was a matter of daily dramas and daily solutions, taxing the ingenuity of the authoritarian Alda and of the manager Geremia Gioffredi. Even before the departure of Berenson and Nicky, some measures had been taken to protect the library and the collection. The most treasured pictures had been packed and sent to the Serlupi villa, while—to avoid tell-tale gaps on the walls—lesser paintings, and even a few engravings, had been distributed to replace the hidden masterpieces. Many books had also gone to Le Fontanelle, where they supplied Nicky and Berenson with reading matter, others to Quarto, villa of Marchesa Ritter, the mother of Marchesa Serlupi. At I Tatti itself, a number of books had been walled up.

The baroness Anrep and Gioffredi dealt with all this concealment and replacement, while Mary, lying upstairs, had taken a dramatic turn for the worse and required constant professional care. On her occasional "good" days, the young Gioffredi had to carry her from her corner bedroom to the comfortable library, a task he later recalled with a smile, since he was short and slender, while Mary's Junoesque proportions had, if anything, increased in her months of enforced inactivity.

The German authorities were daily threatening to requisition the entire villa, and elaborate preparations had to be made for moving Mary to the Anreps' apartment in downtown Florence in Borgo San Jacopo, near the Ponte Vecchio, an area that would presumably be respected in the event of bombing or shelling. In the end, the Germans requisitioned the more spacious Poggio Gherardo instead, and Mary remained in her room. But a number of smaller paintings were taken to the Anreps' for safety.

Eventually a part of I Tatti was requisitioned, as residence and headquarters for the commanding general Kesselring. A few soldiers slept in the house, as his personal guard. Others tented in the garden, where—at one point—orders were given to dig holes for anti-aircraft emplacements. Hearing about the order, the fearless Alda Anrep sternly bade the soldiers to desist; and recognizing a voice of authority (speaking formal, flawless German), they dropped their shovels at once.

On 10 December 1943, three months to the day from their abrupt abandonment of I Tatti, Nicky wrote Mary a long letter describing Berenson's condition, generally good, and their quiet life at Le Fontanelle. Mary replied, some weeks later: "I am very sorry not to write this with my own hand but neither hand nor eyes are working well. The truth is I am dying only I cannot die. The doctors will not give me receipts for medicines that might kill me and I am too ill to go out of my room to look for anything or to die in the garden [. . .] However all this is not important. What I want to express I never could express even if I had the use of my hand and eyes. It is the love and admiration and affection of many years. There is no cloud in the thought of you as there is in almost everything else. [. . .] all is perfectly serene and I think of you with the deepest love [. . .] I am almost glad that B.B. should not see me in my pain and weakness. I love to think how in spite of all our failings and so-called infidelities we have always stuck together and stuck to Italy and when I am able to think at all I think of him with affection."

At the beginning of August 1944, the war of shells and bullets and mines reached Florence. In the night between 3 and 4 August the British Eighth army entered the southern part of the city, on the left bank of the Arno; opposite them, the Germans blew up all the bridges except the Ponte Vecchio. But, to make it unusable, they destroyed all the buildings surrounding its head, and thus Borgo San Jacopo, and the Anreps' apartment, were reduced to a heap of rubble, as the Germans then withdrew to a line at the northern side of the city, stretching directly past the Serlupi villa.

The fighting for the city went on for almost three weeks, during which—when it was possible—the devoted and intrepid Gioffredi, sometimes taking his wife with him, made the hazardous journey from the villa into the city, where they spent long hours amid the rubble of the Anreps' house, seeking out—and finding—fragments of paintings, and taking care that vandals were not around, attracted by the patches of gold from the Sienese *fondi d'oro*.

On 7 August 1944, Berenson wrote in his diary: "Our hillside happens to lie between the principal line of German retreat along the Via Bolognese and a side road reaching the same Via Bolognese after a few kilometres. The Allies are bombarding both these roads and the hill above us as well; for it creeps with parachutists hiding in dug-outs in the wood and keeping their batteries going at the top. We are at the heart of the German rearguard action, and seriously exposed [. . .]

"No news of what is happening in my own place and to my bedridden wife, although they are not two miles away as the crow flies[. . .]

"While this Inferno has been going on, we have been reading Goethe's *Iphigenia*. What a contrast between the noble humanity of this beautiful drama and the bestiality of Hitlerism, both products of the same soil [. . .]"

August 15th: "This is the feast of the Madonna, the most popular holiday of the year. It is the seventeenth or eighteenth day since we have been without electric power, and in consequence without light, without city water, with alarmingly diminishing provisions, and, worst of all, without the radio and the news. The first bit of comfort has just reached us with the sound of church bells that cannot be far away, yet already under Allied occupation;

The art historian Jean Paul Richter sold this painting to Berenson in 1899. Berenson attributed it to the Venetian painter Michele Giambono (active from about 1420–1462). The panel, depicting St. Michael enthroned, hangs in the dining room of I Tatti. It has been dated about 1430. Photo: David Finn

When Berenson acquired this work by the sixteenth-century Sienese artist Brescianino, it had been considerably overpainted and was called simply "Portrait of a Woman." Berenson listed it under that title in 1932. A later restoration revealed the palm in the woman's right hand and the wheel being held against her side. So the anonymous woman was recognized as Saint Catherine. The painting hangs outside the French library. Photo: David Morowitz

Berenson liked, on occasion, to hang pictures against rare fabrics. So this St. Francis—damaged during World War II and restored by G. Marchig—is framed by a piece of eighteenth-century Venetian cut velvet in the living room. Berenson first attributed the work to Gentile da Fabriano then, somewhat hesitantly, to the young Jacobello. The later historian Federico Zeri, also with hesitation, has suggested Paolo Veneziano. Photo: David Morowitz

for since the 'state of emergency,' some ten days ago, the Germans have not allowed them to be rung."

Two days later Berenson and Nicky received indirect word that Mary, the Anreps, and I Tatti were surviving. On the last day of August, friendly visitors began to appear—though the shelling continued around the villa—including a cousin of the Serlupis, then young Contini [Count Alessandro Bonacossi, a collector friend,] in partisan uniform, then the colleague Giovanni Colacicchi, and finally a Major Sampson, head of the Allied office for D.P.'s.

"He will take me over tomorrow afternoon to see Mary and arrange to move me towards the end of next week, bag and baggage, that is to say with the pictures and other works of art, as well as the books I have had here.

"Furthermore he brought the news that he had been to my house, which had been left unharmed by the German occupants and seen my wife, who seems no worse for all we have gone through this past year."

The good news of Mary's health was confirmed by a friend and sometime guest of I Tatti, the conductor Igor Markevitch, who managed to reach the Serlupi villa. The bad news was the condition of the garden, for the population of Ponte a Mensola, the village down the road, had regularly crowded into it for safety during air raids.

The next day, true to his word, Major Sampson sent a car for Berenson and Nicky. Before they could go to I Tatti, the driver had an errand in the city, and so the long-isolated couple were able to see, with horror, the war damage to Florence. When the car stopped, Berenson walked to the Ponte Vecchio: "I doubt whether deliberate havoc like this has been perpetrated before in the course of history. Attila the Hun, and Gaiseric the Vandal, may have had the will but lacked the machinery," Berenson wrote in his diary on 3 September.

Mary seemed "no better for the year, less one week, that has separated us. She was suffering spasms of acute pain, and her speech was clogged," the diary continues. Nicky, who went upstairs separately to visit Mary, recalled that "physically [she was] better than I expected but listless and apparently indifferent [. . .]"

In the car, coming away, Berenson seemed distraught, and Nicky assumed his distress was due to the condition of the house, windowless and pocked by shelling, many trees cut down, soldiers camping in the fields or in the Limonaia.

"That can be remedied," Berenson said, "what I am in despair over is Mary. The moment I entered her room she said that now everything was so changed and the house so heavily damaged she hoped I too would change my mind and give up my foolish plan of leaving it to Harvard University."

This despair apparently contributed to the severe intestinal upset that then kept him at the Serlupi villa for another several weeks. He was too weak to move—at seventy-nine, he finally admitted to feeling old—but strong enough to receive friends and talk with them, always for him a revivifying activity. There were new friends, too: young Allied officers, sometimes

armed with a letter of introduction, sometimes only with their curiosity
and brashness.

It was not until 24 September that Berenson could write: "First morning
at I Tatti. Less than three months ago Serlupi talked of not letting me return
till it was again in apple-pie order exactly as I left it.

"Meanwhile I Tatti has been through the wars [...] the glimpses I

This desk, characteristically
uncluttered, stands in Nicky Mariano's
room on the top floor of the villa.
Photo: David Morowitz

had three weeks ago of its squalid bareness gave me an attack of acute
xenodochiophobia.

"I dare say the polysyllabic word just employed will not be found in dic-
tionaries. I invented it long ago to designate the sinking feeling that in my
travels often overcame me: of fear lest the inn or hotel at which we were to
lodge would be sordid, would not let me have the promised apartment; that
my bedroom would have the wrong proportions, pulling or flattening me
out of my normal shape [...] that the lights would be glaring and no reading lamp by my bed; that there would be sharp or clattering sounds outside,
or bad smells [...]"

Berenson's fears were not unjustified. On 15 October, three weeks after
his return, he wrote: "I cannot settle down satisfactorily for I shall not be able
to remain in my usual apartment. We shall have to shut off those two rooms,
the corridor leading to them, the libraries, all the rest of the house in short,
and huddle into the three guest-rooms small enough to be warmed. I am to

While Berenson attributed this *Entombment* to the workshop of Giotto, many other experts—including, most recently, John Pope-Hennessy—are convinced it is by Giotto himself. The panel belongs to a series depicting stories from the life of Christ; some are in the Alte Pinakothek in Munich, one is in the Metropolitan Museum in New York, and another, acquired through Berenson's mediation, is in the Isabella Stewart Gardner Museum in Boston. Photo: David Morowitz

keep my study as well. Stoves are being put in, hideous terracotta monstruosities in themselves, and ruinous to space-relations and colour-harmony. Nor are we sure as yet of procuring enough fuel for the coming six months. Wood is to be had at no place nearer than over thirty miles by road. It will take $25.00 to fetch it apart from its cost on the spot. By the way, a set of rubber-tyres for a small car costs as much, if to be had. Then there is the difficulty of lighting. With the miserable lamplets available and the foul kerosene, reading is nearly excluded."

But soon Berenson was beginning to count his blessings: his most valuable books and works of art, his collection of photographs—some at Le Fontanelle and some at the Marchese Ritter's Villa Quarto—had survived intact. Only two pictures in the Anreps' apartment had been totally destroyed. No object at I Tatti was damaged.

As always, visitors kept arriving. Berenson, the "passionate sight-seer," to quote the title of an autobiographical volume, had himself become a

Berenson in August 1945 with John Walker, one of the villa's first postwar guests. Courtesy, I Tatti Archive. Photo: David Morowitz

Berenson and Nicky Mariano in the formal garden, in 1941, with the collector Count Contini Bonacossi at left, and a lady identified as Signora Del Giudice at right. Courtesy, I Tatti Archive. Photo: David Morowitz

monument. And so he was to remain. And, though he complained that advancing age had given him a deplorable sense of hurry, he found time to meet and draw out the sight-seers who came to inspect him, as if he were a local landmark.

"No electric current," Nicky wrote later, "[. . .] no bells, the main gate and the house door kept open and at every hour of the day jeeps or army cars would drive up and Allied officers or men would walk in [. . .] others brought up Italian friends who had no transport."

The visitors, Nicky recalled, helped solve the problem of food for the large household; and Berenson himself straightforwardly begged for printed matter in English—impossible to procure during Mussolini's last years—and for news.

Not all of it was good. Many friends were gone. Lady Sybil, anorexic, had starved herself to death in a Swiss luxury hotel. Others had been killed. Still others had remained in exile. But new friends were in the offing, and for that last wartime winter, though he could take no walks in his beloved woods, for fear of German mines, Berenson managed to enjoy the familiar beauty, and pick up the cadence of his old life.

Frederick Hartt, an art historian and U.S. army officer in charge of rescuing and restoring works of art, spent all his free time at I Tatti, and Berenson

followed his work with intense interest. But, as if the semi-silence of his year in hiding had stimulated his ever-present urge to communicate, he began to write. His first effort, produced with Nicky's encouragement, was a selection from his wartime diary. That summer he and Nicky were able to resume their prewar practice of escaping the hot weather in the cool woods of Vallombrosa. There, in the quiet simplicity of the Casa al Dono, an old farmhouse the Berensons had enabled Nicky to acquire, he finished a brief, ruminative autobiography, *Sketch for a Self-Portrait*.

Part of his stimulus to write may have come, unconsciously, from the death of Mary, who had died—with rare serenity—on 23 March 1945. During their early collaboration, when his essential works on Italian art were produced, Mary had never spared criticism of his prose style, insisting on cuts and simplifications, making fun of the purple passages (that reflected Berenson's early love of Pater) and his contorted Germanic sentences.

But Nicky who, like Berenson, spoke English (beautifully) as a second—or perhaps third—language, was expectably more diplomatic and encouraging. And, with Mary gone, Nicky could concentrate all her energies, plus the complementary energies of the Anreps and others of the villa's establishment, to Berenson's comfort and stimulation.

In the early months of his renewed life back at home, he suffered still from the lack of letters—the Italian postal system was not yet functioning—and from the sporadic and not always satisfactory nature of his visitors. Morra, in Rome, managed to send letters via allied officers traveling to Florence. In August of 1945, his long-time friend and correspondent Henry ("Harry") Coster managed to get letters to him from America. From Vallombrosa, Berenson replied: "Please send by post, & do not trust private carriers. Uncertain as posts still are they are much more reliable than private persons [. . .]"

Berenson's great immediate concern was the revitalizing of his library. He was eager to return to his studies, and he was missing all the wartime numbers of specialized scholarly journals. He enlisted Coster's help: "I ask you to help me with publications. I want all of Byzantion & Speculum since 1940. I trust 'second-class mail' will soon be available. At present they might be addressed to Cultural Attaché, *Prof. Morey*, U.S.A. Embassy [. . .]"

In November he wrote again, enquiring about the journals, adding "I am so overwhelmed by visitors, callers, people who come for help & advice, & I am at the same time so greedy for reading that I literally find no time for work [. . .]"

The library began to grow and, by the spring of 1948, another addition was clearly necessary. He got in touch with Cecil Pinsent, who had served in Italy during the war; Berenson had plans for a new wing, to contain a half-a-dozen or so rooms on two floors. And while Pinsent was creating it, he also — probably at Berenson's insistence—considerably revised the fake eighteenth century salottino, a folly of young Geoffrey Scott's, which had always been something of an embarrassment, even before Kenneth Clark dismissed it, in his autobiography, writing of Mary Berenson and Pinsent: "He, and she, were recent converts to the rococo at Nymphenburg, and they had attempted to recreate a room from the Amalienburg, with stucco moldings picked out in apple-green and pink. The result was a ridiculous parody." Now made less coy by the subsequent Pinsent revisitation, filled with bookshelves to house Berenson's personal collection of French literature, it became "the French library," one of the most attractive rooms in the house. Its location, on the ground floor, across a little hall from the dining room, made it an ideal place for intimate meals; and, in fact, Berenson and Nicky usually dined there during his last years, and the director dines there today when the number of guests permits.

Thanks, Berenson suspected, to Nicky's influence, he began seeing more Italians than in the past; and he also made new, younger British and American acquaintances, the poet (and later novelist) Peter Viereck, the journalist Alan Moorehead, Eric Linklater, and the young Welsh art-historian Willy Mostyn-Owen, who came to stay at I Tatti, the latest in the long line of "assistants." Soon old friends were able to return to Settignano: John Walker, Walter Lippmann, a friend since Paris in 1918, John Pope-Hennessy, Mrs. Otto Kahn, and the always-delightful Ruth Draper.

He published not only the *Sketch for a Self-Portrait,* but also, *Aesthetics and History*, a part of what he had hoped would be his culminating work of independent thought, the never-to-be-written Summa. His wartime diaries were ready for publication; but as the immediate postwar interest in him began to wane in English-speaking countries, no publisher seemed willing to take up the project. *Life* magazine published some excerpts in April 1949, part of an article which increased his fame, but aroused no interest in the book. Finally, in the spring of 1951, introduced by John Walker, the American publisher Max Schuster came with his wife to lunch at I Tatti. He asked if Berenson had anything unpublished that might be of interest to him. "Only my war diary," was the reply, "and nobody wants that."

At Schuster's insistence, Berenson allowed him to have the manuscript, which he took back to his hotel. The next day he telephoned Nicky to say "I will not only publish it, I will make a best-seller of it." Under the title *Rumor and Reflection*, it came out in 1952, went through numerous editions, and remains arguably Berenson's most popular book. It is, in fact, an excellent introduction to his mind and his personality, and there are many poignant references to I Tatti.

As time passed, and even his prodigious energies began to ebb, he was more and more confined to I Tatti, and to its summer extension, the Casa al Dono; and his last diaries, *Sunset and Twilight*, published posthumously, record the mellowing of his sharp character.

Many things continued the same. Friends wrote letters: John Pope-Hennessy sent him a running chronicle of cultural events in London; Margaret Scolari Barr (wife of the museum director Alfred Barr) sent a similar chronicle from New York; and Agnes Mongan kept him abreast of news from Harvard. Visitors arrived with increasing regularity, bearing further news of the outside world. And, the more serene Berenson of the last years began the reassuring process of healing old wounds, reconciling with former friend-enemies like his younger—but now aged—colleague and rival Richard Offner, and the brilliant Roberto Longhi, as spiky as Berenson himself.

Some of the friends who came to see him in the last years, realizing that each visit could be the last, tried to sum up and convey to him the importance of his life in theirs. "In the summer of 1955 B.B.'s faculties were unimpaired," Pope-Hennessy writes in his autobiography, "He still [. . .] doff[ed] his nightcap to the new moon. He was (I quote from a letter) "entirely charming, sitting up talking last night till half past eleven and so far

Berenson and Nicky (date uncertain, perhaps in the immediate postwar years) in the *giardino pensile*. Courtesy, I Tatti Archive. Photo: David Morowitz

as one could see not aged in any way." I could scarcely remember him so animated and so funny [. . .]." By the following summer B.B.'s decline was very marked. At I Tatti he was "brought down to the music room to work and deal with correspondence before lunch. You lunch in the French library.

His brain works perfectly, and he hears almost everything one says, but he makes for the first time an impression of great passivity, and is propelled about by a trained nurse who collects him after lunch and supports him upstairs."

Just after New Year's day, 1959, the year of Berenson's death, Pope-Hennessy, returning from a Christmas visit to I Tatti, wrote: "Dearest B.B., I have written to you countless times to thank you for having me at Casa al Dono or at I Tatti, but I think I have never been so conscious as at this Christmas of how great my cumulative debt for all these visits was. They have been an enormously important factor in the last twelve years, and whatever I have done I owe in large part to your influence and encouragement. It is awfully difficult to thank you without recourse to threadbare terms of gratitude, but as each year goes by I am increasingly aware of the depth of my indebtedness [. . .]"

Harold Acton, another close friend, especially in the last years, wrote a parallel letter at about the same time. And, many others harbored similar feelings and expressed them as they could.

Berenson himself obviously had moments of despair, but he also persisted in his plans. On 21 March of 1958, just over a year before his death, he confided to his diary: "I have lost grip in almost every way. I no longer can recall the reasoning by which I arrived at my convictions, particularly in questions of art as experience, and even of attribution. I go on with them, but can no longer discuss them with myself, let alone with others [. . .] Why do I cling to life, despite everything? First and foremost, for Nicky's sake. Then the hope of a younger generation at Harvard that will be better than the present 'art teachers,' and will appreciate what could and should be done with all I Tatti offers them. I continue piling books and periodicals into the library, so as to serve as models for what is to be continued. Of course I cannot hope it will be kept up, as I could afford and my successors may not, even if they had my instinct about books, the fruit of eighty years of experience. One must give oneself reasons for what one does, instinctively or by intuition. How I miss my capacity for justifying my tasks, my convictions, my axioms, my assumptions. [. . .]"

The last year of his life was, as Nicky Mariano later said, "a continual up and down." His best time in the day was in the hour or so after his breakfast, and it was then that he dictated letters and his diary, looked at photographs. At other times, he listened to Nicky—or perhaps to a guest-volunteer—read from what Mary used to call the "sacred" books: *Don Quixote*, the *Decameron*, the *Thousand and One nights*, Trollope, Thackeray. The last book Nicky read to him was *Vanity Fair*.

The southern façade of the villa, with Mary's clock-tower and the enclosed garden. Photo: David Morowitz

Up to the end, friends came: John Walker, Sydney Freedberg, the arche-ologist Doro Levi (victim of the Fascist anti-Semitic laws, now excavating again on Crete), and newcomers like Adlai Stevenson, the Chinese scholar Chen Shi-hsing, introduced by Harold Acton, and—from Harvard—McGeorge Bundy, to reassure Berenson about I Tatti's future.

On the morning of 6 October 1959, the devoted Dr. Capecchi told Nicky that Berenson would probably not live through the day. Asked if she could send for the parish priest for his blessing, Berenson—now reduced to silence—nodded. The priest came and performed his simple duty. That night, Berenson quietly breathed his last, in the house he had created, his home for almost six decades. He was surrounded by those closest to him: Nicky, Alda, Geremia Gioffredi and his daughter Fiorella, his nurses and the house servants.

The next day, shrouded in an ivory-white cashmere shawl, Berenson's body lay in state on the long table in the main room of the library. The farmers, the maids, and the rest of his household were the first to pay their final homage. Then came the authorities, the royal friends, colleagues. After the funeral at the parish church at San Martino a Mensola, the remains were interred in the little chapel inside the gate of I Tatti. Some time later, Mary's coffin was brought down from Settignano, where it had lain for years, and was placed beside his.

Nicky Mariano died in 1968, having lived long enough to see her home of many years transformed gradually and set on its way to becoming the flourishing institution it now is. By her own wish, she was buried not at I Tatti but at the place she probably loved even more, near the Casa al Dono, the house where she and Berenson enjoyed their most serene times, at the simple graveyard of Santa Maria in Alpe, in Vallombrosa. In London, two I Tatti regulars, John Pope-Hennessy and Willy Mostyn-Owen arranged a memorial Mass at the Brompton Oratory; the Victoria Requiem was sung on this occasion.

5

*D*uring Berenson's lifetime, foreseeing an inevitable future without him, Nicky Mariano had acquired the Casa al Dono in Vallombrosa, where she and he spent their summers together. After Berenson's death, she settled with the newly-widowed Alda into a large and hospitable apartment created in the former convent at San Martino a Mensola, below I Tatti and visible from the villa. She lived comfortably and gracefully in her "conventino," which Harold Acton had described as looking like "a lovely old cheese." Very early in Nicky's association with them, the Berensons had—by common accord—invested a sum of money in her name, to assure her future. Through wars and revolutions her family had lost all its money and property abroad, but happily she had no financial worries.

In 1957, the then dean of Harvard, McGeorge Bundy, had an informal conversation with Professor Kenneth Murdock of the English Department, former dean of the faculty and retiring master of Leverett house. Murdock and his wife Eleanor were planning an Italian holiday, and the Harvard authorities thought it would be a good idea if a university representative discussed the future of I Tatti with its ninety-two-year-old occupant. Since Berenson harbored only the greatest distrust of the conventional Ph.D.-producing machine, Murdock suggested, as a model for I Tatti, Harvard's Society of Fellows, an organization of scholars, young but already launched on their careers. In an atmosphere of easy interdisciplinary exchange, they meet at weekly dinners attended also by visiting scholars and university officers. As Eleanor Murdock later recalled, Berenson—suspicious of what he considered the Ph.D. treadmill—concurred, agreeing also that I Tatti's fellows should have an advanced degree or its equivalent.

After Berenson's death, over a year went by before the will was probated and the administrative structure of the Harvard Center for Italian Renaissance Studies could be set up. Somewhat to his own surprise, Kenneth Murdock—experienced administrator but a specialist in American literature, with no Italian—was named the Center's first director, his position to become effective on 1 September 1961. The respected scholar who, until then, had concerned himself chiefly with Cotton Mather was to settle into the house with Sassetta and Signorelli.

In his later diaries Berenson sometimes imagined the future of his house, suggesting even that he would like to haunt it, a benevolent but keen-eyed and not uncritical ghost. Certainly, everyone there felt his presence: the Murdocks, the arriving Fellows, and—some time later—the new librarian, Michael Rinehart, interviewed by Kenneth Murdock in London.

At first, the Fellows were very few in number. Only six, for, in making his will, Berenson had failed to realize that the income on the money he left,

Lunch in the French library with members of the
I Tatti Council visiting from New York. Photo: I Tatti
Archive

Left:

The French library. It was designed by Geoffrey Scott
as a sort of rococo "boudoir" (as Mary described it).
Kenneth Clark made fun of it in his memoirs, and, for
that matter neither Mary nor Berenson liked it, and it
was rarely used. After World War II, when more space
was needed for books, a local carpenter from Ponte
a Mensola (an uncle of the villa's current carpenter)
built the new bookcases. As in Berenson's later years,
it is now used as a second dining room. Photo: David
Morowitz

sufficient to maintain him and the villa in comfortable style, could not be stretched to include fellowships. So, almost as soon as the door of the Center opened, Harvard had to start a fund-raising campaign. The first Fellows—and their hundreds of successors—have always been, to some extent, supported by other institutions: the Guggenheim, the Kress, the Schepp, the Mellon, the Ahmanson, the Florence Gould Foundations, as well as stipends from the Lila Wallace endowment, the Robert Lehman endowment, the Deborah Loeb Brice Fellowship, and, honoring a long-time Berenson collaborator, the Hanna Kiel Fellowship.

When the Murdocks reached the villa, the Italian autumn had already begun; and the empty house was chilly. And as winter came on, the heating of the house—and of bath-water for the guests—became a major concern, since, on the one hand, the Murdocks had to spend a considerable amount of money to re-equip the rooms and, on the other hand, the director was expected to institute a number of economies in carrying out his mandate from Harvard.

Harvard had inherited not only a property, but also a living, human wealth. Moving here, the Murdocks found a long-established, impeccably trained staff headed by Geremia Gioffredi, who had ably managed the estate for over three decades, and had successfully protected I Tatti all during the German occupation and the wartime disruptions. His young daughter Fiorella, in the process of getting her degree, was already at work in the library, where she would eventually become curator of the Fototeca and the Berenson archive. The scrupulous Gino drove the villa's stately Lancia, and the gardeners, the cook Nello, and the farmers were all a part of the household that welcomed the new director and his wife.

On their arrival, Nicky Mariano was there to receive them, symbolically handing over the keys to the house where she had lived and tactfully reigned for forty years. She had already moved into her spacious apartment in the former cloisters of the church of San Martino, where Berenson's funeral had been held. The move cannot have been easy for her, though the change-over must have been long expected. With her usual grace, she concealed any pain she may have felt as she introduced the Murdocks to the staff and showed them over the house.

Diplomatically, the Murdocks did not take over Berenson's bedroom or study; they stayed first in the so-called "Ritz," the guest suite occupied by Edith Wharton, the king of Sweden, and other "A" list visitors. Despite the beguiling (and probably ironical) name given the suite by the Berensons, its rooms are a bit dark; and after a short time, the Murdocks chose to settle into the corner bedroom suite that had been Mary Berenson's, enhanced by an open loggia with a view towards Florence. Successive directors have continued to occupy this suite.

While Nicky quietly guided the Murdocks through the day-to-day organization of the house, her more outspoken sister the baroness Alda introduced Eleanor to some of the mysteries of Florentine life, academic and

Entrance to the Biblioteca Berenson.
Photo: David Finn

social. Though Berenson until his very last years saw many, many people, there were still some people he firmly did not see. Even for Florentine outsiders, however, he represented an august, imposing presence; and once the villa was empty of it, Florence was suddenly full of authorities on how I Tatti should be run (years later, a similar phenomenon occurred when, inspired by Berenson's example, Sir Harold Acton left his villa to New York University). While within their new domain at I Tatti the Murdocks were well received by their staff, their collaborators, and their Fellows, they encountered, in Florentine society, a certain hostility. Some of this was perhaps an inherited, unadmitted hostility towards Berenson himself; and some of the former outsiders now assumed a posthumous intimacy, calling him casually "B. B." whereas, in his lifetime, they would have not dared call him anything but "Mr. Berenson." Some of these newly-acquired friends, and some of Berenson's genuine, but misguided, friends thought that in deriding the Murdocks they would somehow ingratiate themselves with Nicky and Alda. This did not happen. Many Florentines and visitors to Florence objected—and continue to object—to the limited and rigidly observed visiting hours to the villa and the garden, ignoring the fact that I Tatti is private property, a place of quiet study, not a tourist attraction. Enforcing and explaining this situation was often one of Kenneth Murdock's least agreeable duties. Once he emerged from his office (formerly Nicky's, which he took over at her suggestion), with a broad smile on his usually sober, professorial mien: an insistent American tourist had demanded admission to the villa, because he was, he asserted, "a good friend of Bennie Berenson."

The general transformation of what had been a more-than-comfortable private residence into an institution required a number of smaller, domestic changes, some of them, for Nicky, no doubt heart-wrenching. To create more space in the living room, the pianola was given away to a grateful local school; a somewhat macabre, glaring-white plaster cast of Berenson's hands was quietly removed from the living room by Mrs. Murdock, only to reappear mysteriously in its habitual place.

Within a few days, guests began to arrive. Harvard friends, at first, like the historian Giorgio De Santillana and his wife, then the art conservator at the Fogg Museum; gradually other regulars from the past came to the Center for a visit: the Swedish scholar Axel Boethius, the historian of science Alistair Crombie, the great expert on Renaissance drawings Philip Pouncey, the authority on Renaissance fortification John (later Sir John) Hale, Umberto Morra, Agnes Mongan, Iris Origo.

Then, as now, the Fellows generally lunched at the villa, with an afternoon break for tea: but every month or so the director played host to the Fellows, inviting any distinguished guests of the villa to join them, and usually inviting also some Florentine scholar or authority. Though the setting—and the dress—were formal, the tone of the conversation was generally fluent and informed, creating very much the learned atmosphere that Berenson had in mind when making his bequest. The formal weekly Fellows' dinners, in the style of the meetings of Harvard's Society of Fellows—from which wives were excluded—were not popular (with husbands or wives). The Murdocks' successors, Myron and Sheila Gilmore, eliminated the exclusions and most of the formality, while maintaining the level of friendly scholarly interchange.

The amount of work done by those pioneering Fellows was impressive, and was to set the standard for subsequent generations of scholars at I Tatti. The straitened funds available to Harvard served, in a way, these scholars' purposes, for they had the library practically to themselves. Shortly after Michael Rinehart's arrival, an assistant librarian from Harvard came for a three week consultation, also with Alda Anrep, who virtually knew each book personally. A program of acquisition was worked out. The library, from its fifty thousand volumes at Berenson's death, began its steady growth to the one hundred thousand volumes of today.

Very early in the Center's life, the process for choosing Fellows was established. In the latter part of January, when the Director can more easily take some time off from the villa, he travels to Cambridge, where he meets the Center's Advisory Committee, a group of perhaps fifteen scholars, some academics, some curators, one editor. In a quiet, private room on the upper floor of the Harvard Faculty Club, the group sits around a table and sets to work.

"You can hardly see the food," Walter Kaiser describes the lunch, "because of the applications. The place looks like a paper factory after an explosion."

Each applicant—several months before the meeting—must send the committee a curriculum vitae, a research project, and three letters of recommendation. The most recent harvest of applications numbered ninety-one. Each was carefully photocopied and sent out to all the members of the committee, who then brought the papers along to the Harvard meeting.

Obviously, the applicants are all on a high level, and selection is a slow and much-pondered job. Contrary to what might be believed, applicants from Harvard are not advantaged (Kaiser recently calculated that, out of four hundred and fifty admitted fellows, only twenty had been appointed directly from Harvard); and there has been an increasingly numerous representation from countries outside the United States, including scholars from Eastern Europe. There are no disciplinary quotas, either. In a given year, if three exceptional applicants are musicologists, then there may be three musicologists among the Fellows. If none seems outstanding, there will probably be none. The committee does work towards an interesting interdisciplinary mixture; but if at the same time, they find two or three young scholars venturing into adjacent fields, they will try to admit all three so that each can have that special I Tatti benefit of shared discovery and reciprocal encouragement.

The choice is usually made in a single afternoon, but, as Kaiser says, "it tends to be a very long afternoon." But then, the choices made in those hours will condition the life of the villa and of its director—and, most of all, of the future Fellows—for at least a year afterwards.

In Berenson's day, there had been friendly relations between I Tatti and other foreign institutions in Florence like the British Institute (his younger friend Harold Acton had been among its founders) and, especially the Kunsthistorisches Institut, whose wartime director had secretly conspired with Berenson to save I Tatti's treasures from the greedy tentacles of the bulldozing collector Air Marshal Hermann Goering.

Kenneth Murdock paid official calls on Prof. Ulrich Middeldorf of the German Institute and on Ian Greenlees of the British Institute. I Tatti was regularly represented at Florentine official events, the endless centenaries and commemorations that punctuate every Italian year; and, once they were installed at the Center, the Murdocks wisely invited the mayor of Fiesole—under whose jurisdiction the villa lies—to an impressive lunch. Not long thereafter the tediously dusty unpaved road outside I Tatti's wall was helpfully paved, although many pre-luncheon appeals over the past years had gone unheeded.

A good rapport between the Harvard Center and the city of Florence has remained a goal of I Tatti and its directors. Sometimes diplomacy has led to positive achievements; sometimes surprising results were acts of God.

6

The summer of 1966 was particularly dry in Tuscany, so in late October, when it began to rain, the first reaction of the population was grateful relief. But as the rain persisted, day after day, heavy and relentless, that gratitude turned first to uneasiness, then to outright alarm. What is now known usually as "the Florence flood" — though its damage was widespread, from the Tyrrhenian area of Grosseto to Venice and the Adriatic—still caught most Florentines, especially those in authority, by surprise, unprepared.

Safe on its hill, well north of the Arno, I Tatti was rain-soaked, but untouched by the angry waters of the flood. All the same, Myron Gilmore—then director of the Harvard Center for just a year—and his wife Sheila followed the advance of the disaster with concern and frustration. There had never been a television set in the villa in Berenson's day, and even to listen to the radio, Nicky and Bernard had to go into the kitchen to hear the news over the set installed for the staff. But now, in grim black-and-white, all the villa's inhabitants could judge the terrible reality that was threatening the life of the city and—to the horror of the whole, watching world—an irreplaceable part of the cultural patrimony of Western civilization. Along with scenes of smashed cars and submerged bridges, the newspapers ran photographs of the rare books of the Biblioteca Nazionale, parchment pages glued together by the mixture of heating oil, escaping from swamped basements, and mud carried from the upper valleys of the river and its tributaries. When the waters began to recede, there were pictures, too, of smeared paintings. And the Cimabue crucifix in the church of Santa Croce, ruined beyond complete repair, became a symbol of the flood, as a screaming child, caught by a photographer, would come to stand for all the horror of Vietnam.

While the government was criticized for being slow with relief, the art world—nationally and internationally—went into action; the foreign-born residents of Tuscany also were quick to lend a hand. Berenson's old friend Iris Origo promptly set up an organization to assist the Florentine craftsman in the Oltrarno district, many of them wiped out by the disaster, while the international world of art historians and curators devised the mechanisms to provide concerted, coordinated aid.

For the Florentine part of that aid I Tatti became a focal point. In residence were a number of experts—among them Millard Meiss, Frederick Hartt (Berenson's wartime friend), and Frederick Licht. While it was impossible to reach the authorities of the Sovrintendenza by telephone, I Tatti's phones were miraculously in working order. Thus the Renaissance art historian Sydney Freedberg at Harvard, could call Myron Gilmore, an old friend and colleague, and give messages to be relayed to the director of the

Florentine Fine Arts administration. "Ask them," Freedberg would say, "if they can use thirty restorers of painting and twenty restorers of sculpture." And Freedberg would have in hand the list of American volunteers, ready to take off for Italy. Unfortunately, all too often the offer—at least in part—had to be rejected, because in Florence there were simply no accomodations for

A scholarly occasion in the Myron and Sheila Gilmore Limonaia, summer of 1994. In honor of Gino Corti, experts gathered for a symposium on Florentine archival research. The guests included Professor F. W. Kent of LaTrobe University in Australia (at the lectern), and—at the table—panel members Professor Frank d'Accone of UCLA, Dean Malcolm Campbell of the University of Pennsylvania, Professor Gene Brucker of the University of California at Berkeley, Professor Laura Stern of the University of North Texas, and Laurie Fusco, of the J. Paul Getty Museum. Photo: I Tatti Archive

visitors, however badly they were needed. Many devoted experts came anyway and fended for themselves.

In addition to a working telephone, I Tatti also had hot water, so many art experts—grimy after a day in the muck—would come to the villa to clean up. The historian Myron Laskin recalled recently: "Sheila would send a message to invite you to dinner, and there would be a PS: come half an hour early, if you want a hot bath." — an offer few refused.

Presentation of the Fellows' research projects at the beginning of the academic year. Photo: I Tatti Archive

Through the art historian Eve Borsook, a friend of the Gilmores, I Tatti also assumed its special salvaging task. On the morning after the flood, the Sovrintendente Ugo Procacci called Dr. Borsook and asked her help: the fragile glass negatives from the Gabinetto Fotografico of the Uffizi, all caked with mud, had to be washed urgently. Dating back to the 19th century, the Uffizi collection—in the words of Gilmore's later report to Harvard—

is "a comprehensive record of all the works of art in the province of Tuscany, and includes very important documentary photographs of recent restorations."

Urging her cantakerous little car to its utmost, Borsook collected as many negatives as the vehicle would hold and—having called Myron Gilmore in advance—drove her cargo to I Tatti, where the astonished Gilmore appeared on the balcony of his room in his striped pyjamas, to watch as the negatives were delicately unloaded. At the time, no one had any idea how many of the negatives there were: in the end they proved to number around thirty thousand. With the advice of a radiologist from Florence's Careggi hospital, the bath began. Everyone from I Tatti lent a hand: house staff, gardeners, Fellows. Other volunteers came up from the stricken city. "We washed them in the bathtubs," Nelda Ferace, then Myron Gilmore's secretary recalls, "and even in the Limonaia, where there were great old terra cotta jars, meant to hold olive oil." The slides were gently dipped and cleansed, then laid out to dry. "They were all over the steps of the garden, along the walls, the corridors, everywhere. It went on for over a week." Somehow the kitchen managed to provide some kind of lunch for the hard-working washers.

Until recently, if a visitor opened the coat-closet door under the main staircase of the villa, he would find dozens of pairs of rubber boots, the flood-time equipment of the special guests who crammed the house in those winter months of 1966.

As heat and light remained precarious down in the city, I Tatti also became a convenient rallying-place, ideal for the inevitable consultations and meetings needed to coordinate the recovery effort. Fiorella Superbi remembers one day, in particular, when there was to be an important meeting of American and British experts with Luciano Berti, the head of the Bargello museum, and Umberto Baldini, director of the restoration institute of Tuscany. "There was no transport, and so every car at I Tatti was commandeered and sent over to the Pensione Bencistà in Fiesole, to collect the experts." Another observer was reminded of the Paris taxis streaming to the Marne half a century earlier.

Freedberg also organized an air-lift of big drying-machines, necessary for saving the thousands of books and documents from the Biblioteca Nazionale and the Archivio di Stato. To coordinate all of this activity an organization known as CRIA (for Committee to Rescue Italian Art) was born, with I Tatti as its Florentine headquarters. In addition to housing as many of the experts as possible, I Tatti also made initial grants for the most urgent needs, until finally CRIA found an office in the Pitti Palace. CRIA, in turn, generated the still very active Save Venice movement. When CRIA itself closed down, as things returned to normal, the residue of its funds was donated to I Tatti as fellowship money.

The crisis situation in Florence during that winter continued for about four months. Before it was over the writer Francis Steegmuller, who had spent much time at I Tatti some years earlier while working on his biography of James Jackson Jarves, was sent back to Florence to write a report on the flood and its aftermath for *The New Yorker*. His wife, the writer Shirley Hazzard, who accompanied him, recalls the atmosphere of tireless, selfless, purposeful activity. While Sheila Gilmore was then spending much of the day downtown, collecting and distributing blankets and food and other material necessities, Myron was the driving force of a large team of curators and conservators who had come to the city to advise and collaborate. "Every day," Shirley Hazzard recalls, "there was always a long table of international authorities there for lunch, provided by the totally committed staff."

Many of the experts—both Italian and foreign—also visited the Fototeca, where they could find documentation of what this or that work of art had looked like before the flood had inflicted its disfiguring damage. Often a unique old photograph could serve as guide in a complicated process of restoration.

In sum, the disastrous flood had a positive result, too, for I Tatti. Previously considered by many Florentines as an exclusive ivory tower, the villa at last was recognized as a vital component of the city's intellectual life. And the closer association between the Center's Fellows and the leading figures in the world of Italian art and scholarship, a goal of I Tatti since the very beginning of Harvard's direction, became an important and long-lasting reality.

Although the flood necessarily curtailed some of I Tatti's normal activities (and the resident scholars, inevitably and willingly, found themselves involved in the work of salvage), there were still some lectures and a concert during the year, and an important building project—despite a hiatus of more than two months—was satisfactorily completed. The Berensons' old garage was converted into a much more capacious and comfortable space for housing the Fototeca, and in the enlarged area a number of studies could be created for Fellows in addition to a ground-floor reading room. On the upper floor of the library, thanks to a gift from Gordon and Elizabeth Morrill, there was room for a new music library, now named after the donors.

7

*T*he first publication sponsored by the Harvard Center for Italian Renaissance Studies was, appropriately, an Inventory of the Berenson correspondence preserved in the Berenson archive. The volume was scheduled to appear in 1965, marking the centenary of Berenson's birth, and the Inventory was patiently put together by Nicky Mariano, with the help of Fiorella Superbi Gioffredi (now curator of the Archive) and Henry Coster, one of Berenson's most faithful and treasured correspondents. At first sight, the unassuming book might seem hardly more than a list of names; but actually, a closer study of those names indicates not only the extraordinarily vast range of Berenson's circle of acquaintance, but even more, the apparently boundless extent of his interests.

In his report to Harvard's president the following year, Myron Gilmore wrote: "It is the hope of all those connected with the administration of the Center that a regular program of publication can be undertaken in the future. There are now more than fifty scholars who have been Fellows or Associates of I Tatti [. . .] Many of them have materials—documents discovered or interpretative essays—which were the result of their researches during their tenure of the fellowship. An annual volume of studies and documents perhaps centered in successive years on the different special fields of art history, history, or literature in which the Fellows have worked would provide an appropriate outlet for the publication of their work and make a contribution to Renaissance studies."

This program was still in the planning stage when Myron and Sheila Gilmore left I Tatti in 1973, after supervising nine years of fruitful growth and stabilization. Thanks, in part, also to the terrible flood of November 1966, the Harvard Center was an established part of the Florentine intellectual panorama. The number of fellows had increased, and more and more, the library and the Fototeca were being used profitably by local scholars.

Gilmore's successor had been chosen some time before, and—for the first time—the director had not come from the ranks of the Harvard faculty. A graduate of Princeton, Craig Hugh Smyth had been for twenty-two years director of the Institute of Fine Arts of New York University. He was no stranger to I Tatti, having worked there as a young scholar, with Berenson's encouragement and friendship. In moving to Florence and taking over the guidance of I Tatti, Smyth knew he could count also on the active, thoughtful collaboration of his wife Barbara, who would be, as always, his partner in this new venture.

Among Craig Smyth's goals was the activation of the publications program, but before he could deal with that he was faced by severe practical problems. Since Berenson's death, I Tatti had never been, economically speaking, a going concern. At the Institute one of his less enjoyable (though highly successful) occupations had been fund-raising. The Harvard authorities had assured him that, at the Center, he would be concerned only with running the place and fund-raising would be done through Cambridge.

But, coinciding with Smyth's arrival, Italy suffered a grave financial crisis; inflation was rampant, but the official value of the dollar was maintained, and Smyth rightly refused to exchange Harvard's dollars on the black market (the fashionable Florentine banker who advised him otherwise eventually went to jail). For I Tatti, a huge debt was looming, and for the Villa's employees—their fixed salaries fast losing purchasing power—the situation was parlous.

"Myron had, quite wisely, just made the farmers no longer share-croppers, but employees," Smyth recalls, "with perfectly appropriate salaries, when they were established, but then—almost abruptly—insufficient for a family to live on." So as the new director, Smyth decided immediately to raise the farmers' salaries.

The Fototeca.
Photo: David Morowitz

And then, despite all his best intentions and Harvard's reassurances, he found himself fund-raising. Since seeking money in Boston was awkward, because of the proximity of other Harvard money-seekers and patrons, Smyth chose to concentrate his activity in New York, where he founded the I Tatti Council—an active and fruitful organization that continues to provide support, not only financial, to the Center. It was then that, thanks to

Smyth's powers of persuasion and to the assistance of Council members Edwin Weisl and, in particular, Barnabas McHenry, lawyer to the Lila Acheson Wallace Foundation, the Foundation began its association with I Tatti, which has played an important role in the Villa's existence, especially with its permanent funding of the garden.

As an art historian with a long and distinguished career behind him, Craig Smyth—more than the literary scholar Kenneth Murdock or even the historian Myron Gilmore—found himself at home at I Tatti, among colleagues of old acquaintance, and former students, and rising young scholars. He and Barbara were able to consolidate the achievements of their predecessors and put an enduring structure on the solid foundations they had laid. With the Smyths' tenure, the Harvard Center came into sharper focus, taking on more or less the distinct personality that has been enriched and developed by Smyth's successors.

Among the fellows Smyth found on his arrival was the art historian Charles Dempsey, who happened to show the new director a review he had just written. Smyth recalls saying to him: "That's not a review, that's a book." And so the Center's Publications Program was revived, and—in 1977—Dempsey's monograph *Annibale Caracci and the Beginnings of the Baroque Style* was published, under I Tatti's auspices, by the J. J. Augustin Verlag in Gluckstadt; and a year latter, another Fellow's seminal work, *Masaccio: the Documents,* by James Beck was brought out again by Augustin, now relocated in the United States.

Then the proceedings of two conferences in 1976 and 1977—on *Florence and Venice: Comparisons and Relations*—organized by Smyth with Sergio Bertelli and Nicolai Rubinstein were published in two volumes in 1979–80 by La Nuova Italia, a distinguished Florentine house.

In 1985, the first volume of *I Tatti Studies: Essays in the Renaissance* appeared, edited by the Florentine priest-scholar Salvatore Camporeale and the Australian historian F. W. Kent, with Caroline Elam. Elam, Camporeale, and Kent have remained active in the direction of the biennal series, collaborating with the art historian Elizabeth Cropper and, ex officio, with the directors of the Center Louise George Clubb (1985–88) and Walter Kaiser, who has guided I Tatti from 1988 to the present. The five volumes so far published indicate forcefully the range of interests explored by the scholarship at I Tatti.

The departure of Myron Gilmore was marked by a Festschrift volume of essays. Similarly, two volumes of *Renaissance Studies in Honor of Craig Hugh Smyth* were edited by Andrew Morrogh, Fiorella Superbi Gioffredi, Piero Morselli and Eve Borsook, the first volume devoted to History, Literature and Music, while the second concentrated on Art and Architecture. Shortly before the death of Sir John Pope-Hennessy, a collection of his reviews—celebrating his eightieth birthday—was edited by Michael Mallon and Walter Kaiser. The volume included several reviews concerning Berenson, his writings and—in particular—a closely-argued and sometimes characteristically caustic defense of Berenson's reputation against the inaccurate slurs of some irresponsible writers.

During Berenson's lifetime, a project was initiated, to document the holdings of I Tatti in published form. A somewhat cursory catalogue of the collection at I Tatti was issued in Milan in 1962. Eventually, a more thorough catalogue will have to be prepared. In the meanwhile, one area of the collection (not covered in the Milan publication) has been catalogued in an exemplary fashion by Laurance Roberts. This is the Oriental Collection, a small but exquisite assembly of works of art that were particularly dear to their owner and now illuminated by the expertise and insight of Roberts, an old friend of I Tatti.

Italians love celebrations, and birthdays—especially centenaries or multiples thereof—offer splendid occasions for everything from fireworks to art works. The year 1992 was especially rich. The abundance of important anniversaries created the fear that none would be seen in suitably high relief. And there was the fear, too, that official funds would be insufficient, or would be spread too thin. The city of Pesaro naturally wanted to pay special attention to the two hundredth birthday of Gioacchino Rossini; Arezzo and its province insisted on recalling the five hundredth anniversary of the death of the great local son Piero della Francesca; Genoa had mounted a huge Columbian Year in 1892 and felt obliged to repeat—and improve upon— the pomp and circumstance for the five hundredth anniversary of the discovery of America.

In all this kaleidoscope of grandiose celebratory planning, Florence contemplated an anniversary of special local and international meaning: the cinquecentennial of the death of Lorenzo de' Medici. Well in advance of the date, I Tatti decided to arrange a suitable commemoration; but, rather than make a futile and unseemly attempt to monopolize the Magnifico, Walter Kaiser chose to invite Italy's National Institute for Renaissance Studies to participate as an equal partner. At a meeting between Professor Kaiser and the head of the Institute, details were worked out. In broad terms, they decided that I Tatti would organize a conference, and the Institute would publish the Proceedings.

The Harvard Center's four-day international conference was entitled "Lorenzo the Magnificent and His World." For the scholarly committee of advisers, Kaiser could call on an impressive assembly of old friends and frequenters of I Tatti: Nicolai Rubinstein, Cesare Vasoli, Gene Brucker, Domenico De Robertis, Caroline Elam, F. W. Kent, Michael Mallett, Nino Pirrotta, John Pope-Hennessy and Salvatore Settis. From California and Pisa, from Australia, from London, and also from Florence itself, these and other scholars foregathered to examine, from various and stimulatingly different perspectives, that fifteenth century flowering of culture that has motivated culture and cultural studies for half a millennium.

Putting it all together was not an easy job. In Italy, as even the most patriotic Italians will admit, brilliance is easier to find than punctuality. And

The "big" library. This was the first library room designed for Berenson. The space was formerly a barn. It can be reached directly from the second floor of the villa. It is now used also for meetings and, occasionally, for musical events. Photo: David Finn

anyone who has been to a scholarly conference in Italy will be familiar with the absences announced at the last minute, the unfinished papers that turn into disorganized causerie, the twenty-minute speeches that last an hour, the morning sessions that cause lunch to be put back endlessly, and the afternoon sessions that drag on as the chilled aperitifs turn warm and the canapes grow soggy.

Setting aside for a moment the cultural success of the Lorenzo conference at I Tatti, outside visitors, the fellow-travelers of culture, were impressed, not to say stunned by the clockwork efficiency of Kaiser and his staff, all sheathed in a sincerely welcoming cordiality. For three early-June days—after a preliminary, formal inauguration in the Palazzo della Signoria—between two and three hundred people gathered at I Tatti to listen to about thirty speakers report on their various areas of specialization, which could range from the much-debated economic situation of Lorenzo's Florence, clearly outlined by Gene Brucker, to Lorenzo's rapport with the church, cogently investigated by the rising young historian Roberto Bizzocchi, at that time a Fellow of I Tatti.

I Tatti Fellows, for that matter—Charles Dempsey, Melissa Bullard, James Hankins, and at least a dozen others—made up the main body of the Conference speakers, proving, as Kaiser later commented with justifiable satisfaction, that "in any major conference on Lorenzo il Magnifico, most of the leading participants would have to be scholars somehow associated with I Tatti."

The big library set up for an illustrated public lecture. Photo: David Morowitz

The Signorelli corridor, which derives its name from the two portraits by Luca Signorelli of the Vitelli brothers, visible at right, midway along the passage. Photo: David Finn

The Director's office. Photo: David Finn

Another observer remarked the atmosphere that extended to the morning breaks for coffee and the afternoon one for tea. From the airy Limonaia, setting of the speeches, participants and guests would climb up to the terrace for refreshment; and colleagues, fellow-specialists would seek one another out. Here and there, a senior academic—what the Italians call a "baron" — would position himself in a shaded chair and receive his court of admirers, former students, friends.

There were many intangible results, but the concrete result was the publication of the proceedings of the Conference, edited by Gian Carlo Garfagnani for the Florence publisher Leo S. Olschki. The handsome volume, however, cannot convey the real excitement that underlay the meetings. In some ways, the final one was the most exciting and the most unusual. By a decision of the organizing committee, it was open only to the invited participants in the conference, and the purpose was to examine the conference and

This Chinese statue of a monk, dating from about 570 (Northern Qi dynasty), stands in the library (see page 62). Affectionately referred to by the staff as "the Chinese Madonna," the figure may originally have held a scroll in his opened hands. Photo: I Tatti Archive, courtesy of the Gabinetto Fotografico, Sovrintendenza alle Gallerie, Firenze

debate its points. In the so-called "stanza di Lorenzo" in the Palazzo Pitti, after the papers by James Hankins and Patricia Rubin that ended the conference, the discussion ranged at length and widely, proving the vitality of the undertaking, which was—as its organizers intended—the "academic event" of the Laurentian year.

A number of significant conferences, while perhaps less star-studded and less grand, have preceded and followed the great Lorenzo meeting. In 1990,

Opposite:
This Greek terra-cotta figure of a woman, dating from the fourth century B.C., stands in the upper corridor. Photo: David Finn

while he was a fellow at I Tatti, Lucio Riccetti came to the director to suggest an informal round-table on *Opere*. Few laymen have even an idea of what an Opera is, though some may have actually visited the splendid, but almost secret Museo dell' Opera del Duomo in Florence. The Opera was, in effect, the managing body of a large church or cathedral, responsible for the maintainence and improvement of the fabric, for hiring workmen, even commisioning works of art. Responsibilities and formation varied, and in the Tavola Rotonda that ensued at I Tatti, Italian and foreign scholars discussed the Opere of Pisa, Siena, Orvieto, Florence, Milan, Bologna, Venice, and elsewhere. The consequent volume—edited by Riccetti and Margaret Haines and seen through the press by Fiorella Superbi Gioffredi—is anticipated from the printers as these words are being written. It promises to be an invaluable work to scholars in fields ranging from architecture to city-planning, from economics to sociology.

A similar Conference, devoted to Aldus Manutius and organized by I Tatti in collaboration with the university of Venice, has also brought together and put in order an immense amount of knowledge concerning the great sixteenth century Venetian printer and humanist. And while more social citizens are already ordering the champagne for their end-of-the-millennium parties, I Tatti is planning a conference to be held in 1999, which will examine retrospectively Renaissance scholarship in the 20th century. No one will be surprised to see, again, the huge role played by I Tatti—first as Berenson's home and then as the Harvard Center's—in that immense corpus of learning.

*I*n the autumn of 1929, when Berenson was preparing to set off on a tour of the Middle East, he consulted Lewis Levy, the Duveens' lawyer, about the making of his will and Mary's. Having provided already for the members of his own family and for Mary's, Bernard arranged to leave his property and funds for the founding of his "Instituootion," as Mary contemptuously called it. Mary could only protest so much, but in a letter to Nicky, she unburdened her resentments: "I do not see my way to change anything as B.B. does not recognize that I had any share in building up his career, though indeed without me in the beginning he would have drifted and never written a line . . . Alas that all the money goes into the cursed Institute."

The 1929 will inevitably underwent revisions, especially after Mary's death. The final redaction—in English, but on Italian official-document paper, *carta bollata da L. 200*—decreed, after a bequest to Nicky—"I give, bequeath and devise all of my real estate and interests in real estate including the premises known as I Tatti, situated in the Parish of San Martino a Mensola, in the cities of Florence and Fiesole, Italy, together with all of the furniture, household goods, automobiles, ornaments, fittings, library, books, documents, photographs, pictures, paintings, and objects of art situated at said I Tatti to THE PRESIDENT AND FELLOWS OF HARVARD COLLEGE [. . .] absolutely and forever [. . .]

"My primary purpose in making this bequest of the property [. . .] is to further, under the supervision of the Department of Fine Arts at Harvard, research and education in Italian art and in the Mediterranean world as centered in Italy and focused in Greco-Roman-Byzantine-Italian art, along the line to which I have devoted my life. It is my desire to provide facilities for study and research for the benefit of those who wish to study art visually rather than the technique of its creation, in order that they may acquire a more complete understanding and appreciation of the humane spirit and of the aesthetic genius as manifested in artistic creation and achievement. My ideal is that they should become ripe humanists and not mere teachers of facts about the arts.

"To that end I whish [sic] the property at I Tatti to be maintained as an institute for mature students intending to be sholars [sic] in art and who are eager and able to devote several years abroad in studying the artistic achievements of past epochs in Mediterranean civilization, especially in Italy. I do not mean it to be a work-shop for the petty and parochial study of Italian art, nor is it my purpose to provide a school for the training of painters and sculptors; I should wish those students to have the privilege of dividing their time between travel and residence at I Tatti."

Further Berenson insisted that the students accepted at I Tatti should come not only from the United States and England (he envisioned the eventual collaboration of Cambridge and Oxford), but that the library should be open, free of charge, for all students of Italy and other countries.

From the six Fellows of the first year, 1961, the number of students nominated to I Tatti annually has stabilized at fifteen. In addition to the "borsisti" as they are called (*borsa* in Italian means purse or, here, stipend), there are also intermittent visitors, and more mature scholars formally associated with the Center.

In recent years, Fellows have been asked, on leaving I Tatti, to write a few pages, summing up the results of their work at the Harvard Center, their impressions of its functioning, and suggestions for change and improvement. Among the inevitable complaints about the machinery—the printer, the photo-copiers—common to just about every library in the world, there were many useful indications of the library's strong areas and of those which could be further strengthened. But, from almost all the reports, many sent from foreign universities after the Fellows' return to their normal base and their regular academic duties, there rises a chorus of praise, tinged with surprise (almost all the visitors seem to have found something different, greater than what they expected), and—even after an interval of a few weeks—nostalgia and a yearning, an expectation of return. A typical, recent report concludes: "The intellectual exchange among the fellows was very valuable both in terms of finding out more about my own field and in terms of broadening my knowledge of other fields with which I have seldom . . . had the leisure or the opportunity to become familiar [. . .] Having an intellectual exchange that shakes one away from comfortable intellectual paths is stimulating and creative [. . .] The contact with their completely different disciplines was of value in terms of my scholarly specialty, but probably had its greatest value in terms of improving teaching. Both of these aspects represent, perhaps, what Berenson had in mind for the program as a bit of leisure in which to have a broadening experience."

Scholars are usually visualized as solitaries, and even Berenson in his mention of the "lay monastery," indicated that his future, posthumous guests should live in cellular isolation. Yet, if ever a scholar was social, it was Berenson himself. And, while as an old man he castigated himself for having written less than he could have, he spent a lifetime communicating his ideas verbally. Standing in front of his Domenico Veneziano Madonna, he would expound joyfully to some mesmerized guest the distinction between outline and contour.

And, in their reports, I Tatti's present-day scholars express their satisfaction not only with the work they have accomplished in their time in Settignano, but also with the communication they have had with fellow-investigators and with Florentine or Italian colleagues.

There have always been visiting lecturers at the Harvard Center and, at irregular intervals, the resident Fellows have reported—to their peers in the villa—in a more or less formal way on the progress of their research projects. But, in the past, some have complained that the audience for these oral reports was too specialized; it was often a matter of preaching to the converted, while a more interdisciplinary approach would be fruitful.

A successful step in this direction has been taken with the institution of the seminars or round tables. These vary in scope: the round table discussions are deliberately confined to small, working groups of fifteen or twenty participants, practically without audience. The larger seminars, on broader themes, may attract several hundred people.

A typical large seminar, held a year or so ago, was entitled "Ritual and Meaning," a subject proposed by Giovanni Ciappelli, an Ahmanson Foundation Fellow, who coordinated the two sessions, morning and afternoon, that allowed the reading of six papers in fields ranging from musicology to history, literature, and art history. Ciappelli himself contributed a paper on "Carnival Fights and Lenten Peaces," a product of his I Tatti stay. The visiting professor Timothy McGee, from the University of Toronto, spoke about "Ceremonial Music and the Musicians who Performed." What pleased the participants most was the probing discussions after each session.

Earlier that year, the subject of "Rhetoric and Writing," proposed by Marina Beer, an Italian Fellow, with the assistance of another Italian scholar at I Tatti, Riccardo Spinelli, generated a particularly interesting round-table, involving several students of Italian Renaissance literature. In all, a group of about twenty specialists read papers or discussed them. And Ingrid Rowland illustrated how the concept of "architectural order" can be considered a reelaboration of the Latin term "genus," citing Alberti, Raphael, and Angelo Colucci. Salvatore Camporeale, a long-time habitué of I Tatti and a Research Associate, summed up the findings of the assembled scholars.

But much disciplinary line-crossing was effected over lunch, or tea, or during strolls in the garden, when one colleague would offer a bibliographical nugget to another, or be asked, in turn, to check a Latin translation. In many instances, the scholars used I Tatti as a home base, venturing to libraries and archives in other cities, or exploring—as Berenson and Mary had done a century ago—the dim and dusty churches of little Tuscan towns, to verify the description of an obscure altarpiece, or to study, in situ, the irregular shape of a Romanesque shrine.

*I*t is exactly three P.M. on a warm, almost summery mid-October afternoon. In the large room in the library—where Edith Wharton delighted in "browsing at all hours" — the lights are on, the great upholstered sofa and the seductively comfortable leather chairs have been shifted against the walls; and in the center, lighter chairs have been arranged around the long table. Smaller chairs have been unfolded and placed in two wider, elliptical rows around the table. The room is nearly full.

At the head of the table Walter Kaiser, the Harvard Center's fifth director, is already seated; and this year's fellows have taken their places around the table. One, Michael Segre from the Ludwig-Maximilian University in Munich, will remain absent: he has been excused so that he can attend a scientific conference in Udine. Another, Jérôme Hayez from the Sorbonne, has apparently lost track of time, at work upstairs in his study. He arrives, apologetic, slightly out of breath, and takes his seat, and the meeting can get under way.

It is a relaxed, and yet solemn occasion. The academic year at I Tatti is about to begin, and—following a custom initiated by Craig Smyth and amplified by Walter Kaiser—the new Fellows will be introduced to the staff, the Visiting Professors, and the Research Associates—and to one another. To reduce the tension still further, Kaiser makes a few quotidian announcements. Some of the Fellows have already been at I Tatti for a week or so; but many are here today for the first time. So the director explains some of I Tatti's ways, and some of Harvard's expectations.

First of all, a practical matter of transportation; a shuttle bus, at regular intervals on weekdays, will bring the scholars from their working places in the city—Biblioteca Nazionale, Archivio di Stato, Kunsthistorisches Institut—up to the villa. Berenson's will and Harvard policy encourage the young scholars to get out of their studies and pursue their research among first-hand sources, to go and look at pictures and sculptures and buildings. But they are asked also to come back to the base for lunch at least three times a week; they are encouraged, too, to bring guests, including spouses or visiting colleagues, or newly-made Italian professional acquaintances.

"I will have guests frequently myself," the director goes on to say. "Often these visitors will be patrons of I Tatti, the people who contribute funds to allow the Institute to continue and to improve." As a rule, these supporters are eager to meet the beneficiaries of their largesse, so Kaiser asks the Fellows to introduce themselves to such visitors, and to help entertain and enlighten them.

The Fellows are asked also to make a note of any books they may need that are not in the library collection. Within the realm of possibility, the

Arches leading to the kitchen courtyard. One of the corridors joining the villa to the library runs above the arches. Photo: David Finn

Center will then acquire the books. "You will be doing us a favor," Kaiser says, "helping us complement and enrich our holdings."

Part of the experience of I Tatti is the enjoyment of a hospitality that perpetuates the Berenson tradition. The fellows, at the villa, do not only encounter books, photographs, documents, but also a staff who have long been associated with the place (some were even born on the property, some are sons and daughters of former I Tatti staff). So the director asks the long-standing members of the I Tatti family to identify themselves: the librarians, the administrators, who will be helping the scholars find a required publication, or explaining some quirk of Italian bureaucracy (with which they, like all visitors, will have to deal), or dispensing other practical information, about travel, schedules, unfamiliar national holidays.

Kaiser announces that there will be a guided tour of the Berenson collection—or two tours, if it isn't convenient for all the Fellows to be there on a given day—to be conducted by the collection's curator Fiorella Superbi Gioffredi. "Then, when you have guests at the villa and they want to see the pictures, you can at least make a show of being knowledgeable," Kaiser says with a smile.

Finally, the big moment has come. The Fellows, one by one, are to describe their projects briefly (they have five minutes each, and for the most part they remain within their allotted time). The next two hours afford an intriguing cross-section of Italian Renaissance scholarship: one scholar is planning to investigate the Medici residences in Rome between 1587 and 1637, studying not just the Villa Medici and Palazzo Madama, but other palaces that the Medicis bought or built or rented or tried to rent, including one—in Via del Colosseo—which has been closed to the public for decades (she has the shy hope that her I Tatti Fellow status may finally unlock the door, and Kaiser promises support); a French scholar has been studying—and will pursue this avenue—the correspondence of Tuscans who were in the Avignon around 1400, including the "merchant of Prato" portrayed by the late Iris Origo, Berenson's friend. A young professor from St. Louis is investigating the relationship between Shakespeare's clowns and the characters of the *commedia dell'arte*; while a young Italian woman is examining public health resources in cinquecento and seicento Florence, especially the assistance of maternity cases. Sometimes subjects are related: several scholars are concerned with illustration (including a sober young woman who speaks with demure enthusiasm about the erotica of Giulio Romano); others are interested in the theater, whether in texts or in scenery, and its relation to the ideal city. One man is planning an edition of the trecento poet Antonio Pucci, long considered "popular," earthy, and therefore less worthy than the more high-minded authors of the time. A professor of literature describes the difficulty of establishing a trustworthy text of Cardano's *De vita propria*—which is precisely what he plans to do.

Architecture figures in several projects, including one that will investigate the relationship between the conflicting religious ideas in late-sixteenth-

The Director, Walter Kaiser, in the formal garden.
Photo: David Finn

century Italy and the architecture of certain northern Italian cathedrals, notably those of Vercelli, Brescia, and Mantua.

It is five o'clock. Discreetly, at one end of the library, tea has appeared, with plates of the exquisite cakes produced by the villa's kitchen. A brief break allows stretching of legs, particularly appreciated by those who have been on the unfolded chairs rather than in the great leather ones (reserved, rightly, for the more elderly)

When the last of the new Fellows has spoken, the director then explains the purpose of the visiting professors—who are at I Tatti to do their own work, of course, but also to be available for informal consultation by the Fellows—and the two current visitors are introduced: the historians Christine Meek of Trinity College, Dublin, and F. W. Kent of University of Monash, Australia. Professor Meek brings to life the compelling figure of Paolo Guinigi, lord of Lucca for thirty years in the fourteenth century, while Bill Kent records his progress on a biography of Lorenzo il Magnifico, justifying the need for such a book and cogently listing the problems involved in creating it.

The research associates are also older scholars, working in and out of I Tatti on a long-term basis. Again, Kaiser suggests a quick round of self-introduction and progress report: Fabio Bisogni tells of his study of noble Sienese portraiture of the golden days; Lina Bolzoni briefly discusses her research on the relevance of Horace's famous dictum *ut pictura poesis* ("as is painting, so is poetry") to Italian literature between the sixteenth and eighteenth centuries; Eve Borsook tells of new information about the Capella Palatina in Palermo and on the history of mosaic-making.

Several of the scholars—notably Margaret Haines—discussed databases and CD-ROMs in connection with the assembling and ordering of documents (she is chiefly concerned with the Florentine Opera del Duomo at the time of the construction of the cupola, richly documented); and Laura Corti is making a similarly scientific survey of architectonic terms found in treatises of the Renaissance.

"Some subtle, underground links have emerged, I believe," Walter Kaiser says, concluding, "I see several of your projects are related, and I know you will be enriching one another. I urge you, while you are here, to talk among yourselves, to make apparent the community that exists here."

And he summed up: "The thing that makes I Tatti different from other, apparently similar scholarly communities is this, in my opinion: here, all of you—from whatever background you may come—speak the same language: the language of the Italian Renaissance."

The statue and niche that mark the lower end of the formal garden (restored in 1994). Photo: David Finn

The villa seen from the formal garden.
The boxwood is trimmed to the shapes
it had in Berenson's time (see page 99).
Photo: David Finn

Opposite:
The stairs and niche that mark the
upper end of the cypress allée.
The architecture reflects Pinsent's
design later used for the west door
(see page 53). Photo: David Finn

The eastern facade of the villa (at right)
and the access to the cypress allée.
Photo: David Morowitz

This portal of Tuscan *pietra serena* frames the west entrance to the main floor of the villa. It opens into a long, straight corridor whose eastern door is close to the main gate and the Vincigliata road. Photo: David Morowitz

Every year, since the beginning of the Harvard Center's existence, the resident director has, with the arrival of summer and the temporary dispersal of the Fellows, drawn up a report of the year's activities, its achievements, its problems including those solved and those persisting. Not long ago, as the Center was well into its fourth decade of life, at the request of the president's office in Cambridge, director Walter Kaiser also outlined a five-year plan for the Center.

On the first page, after describing the Center's aims (which remain very close to the intentions outlined in Berenson's testament), Kaiser summed up the fellowsip program, which he called "I Tatti's *raison d'être*." At present, fifteen post-doctoral Fellows in the early stages of their careers are welcomed at the Villa, coming from various countries and working in numerous disciplines. They are chosen by an international committee of senior Renaissance scholars, and—according to their need—each Fellow is granted a stipend of up to $35,000. Some are also given free housing on the I Tatti property: none lives in the villa itself, but there are apartments in the Villino across the road, in the hamlet of Ponte a Mensola down the road (including what was once the apartment of Nicky Mariano and her sister Alda); the Villa Papiniana, on the hill above the Villino—once the residence of Berenson's friend, the art historian Roberto Papini—is now also available, usually reserved for a visiting professor with family.

The Fellows are given private studies within the villa and the freedom of the library seven days a week from 8 A.M. to 10 P. M. (at first the library closed at lunch time, but during her directorship, Louise Clubb arranged for it to remain open, winning the gratitude of those researchers who wanted to exploit every waking hour to the utmost). Morning coffee (usually in the comfortably restored Granaio), lunch in the dining room, and afternoon tea, either in the living room or—in fine weather—under the trees above the garden, are provided on weekdays. Fellows are encouraged to invite guests and to introduce them to their colleagues.

Other, older and more established scholars are appointed as Visiting Professors or Visiting Scholars, and are expected to visit the villa at some length and to act as informal advisers to their younger colleagues.

For still longer terms, Research Associates—permanent residents of Florence or the Florentine environs—are appointed. At this writing, for example, they include the art historian Fabio Bisogni of the University of Siena, the professor of literature Lina Bolzoni from the University of Pisa, and the villa's long-time friend Eve Borsook, as well as historian Allen Grieco, who in addition to studying the social and cultural history of food and eating in the Renaissance, also lends a hand in the management of I Tatti's home farm.

Walter Kaiser's view of the Center's immediate future does not contemplate any significant change in the fellowship program, which now has close to five hundred "alumni" in every part of the world. One of the most valuable aspects of becoming a Fellow is that, even after your appointed term is ended, you remain a kind of Fellow-for-life, always welcome at the library and at I Tatti's table. So visitors, from Italy or from abroad, have a scholarly home whenever they are within reach of Florence. As a result of a recent, vigorous campaign, the fellowship endowment has been substantially increased, so the fund-raising effort—while it must necessarily continue—is under less pressure.

Libraries need books, but they also need space. And the Center is thinking ahead. Italy, that land of landmarks, has—understandably—a firm law regarding construction; and on a property like I Tatti, in the heart of the incomparable Florentine hills, new architectural "volume" is sternly forbidden. Fortunately, some of I Tatti's garages and farm sheds can be replaced by the same amount of cubic feet of compact shelving and Fellows' studies. Some extension can also be underground, as in urban libraries elsewhere.

The complexity of Italy's laws (which not even a Harvard law professor could be expected to grasp) affects I Tatti in a number of ways. Benefits paid to employees come to 53% of salary, and severance pay—provided, unlike the American system, to any employee who leaves, voluntarily or involuntarily—is on a much higher scale than in the United States; and since, with the villa, Harvard inherited a rather elderly staff, this entry in the annual budget has been particularly burdensome. The swings of the dollar-lira exchange (I Tatti receives its funding in U.S. currency and spends its income in lire), which so troubled the early months of Craig Smyth's directorate, continue their erratic course, but Walter Kaiser has managed to work out a forward rate contract with the Center's bank, so that the annual budget can be more accurately projected.

Despite continuing financial difficulties, the Center has recently managed to rewire the entire property, in accordance with European Union requirements.

"I Tatti can be seen," Walter Kaiser wrote once, "as the 20th-century realization of the old Renaissance dream of a *locus amoenus*—a congenial place set apart from the quotidian cares, where lively minds can engage in quiet study and fruitful converse. I have also claimed," he continued, "that the sight of two Fellows strolling through the gardens deep in talk is almost a symbol of what I Tatti uniquely offers and, in itself, justifies all Harvard's efforts to preserve this house, its contents, its surrounding landscape, and its life of the mind."

A walkway, opposite the door designed by Cecil Pinsent. Photo: David Morowitz

Path through Berenson's beloved "English meadow," one of his favorite daily walks. The area is rich in wild flowers: species tulips, hellebore, grape hyacinths, as well as daffodils and anemones. Photo: David Finn

The *giardino pensile* seen from
below. Photo: David Finn

The cypress allée seen from
below. It follows, more or less,
the line of the old Via di
Vincigliata, the road that ran
straight up the hill and passed
right in front of what is now
the villa's front door, separating the house from the
chapel. Pinsent and Berenson
succeeded in having the road
moved, causing its present,
wide curve to be made.
Photo: David Finn

⤳ Photographers' Notes

My work for this book has been made possible by the extraordinary kindness of a number of people, who have earned my life-long gratitude. Among these friends are Professor Walter Kaiser, Director of the Harvard Center for Italian Renaissance Studies, who provided unfailing guidance, encouragement, and an occasional iced vodka during my rushed days at work; Dottoressa Fiorella Superbi, who graciously opened the Center's archives for me; Nelda Ferace, who answered each of my many questions with patience and friendliness; Amanda George, a superb photographer, who treated me as an old friend met after long absence; Susan Bates, who made "all the arrangements" to make my arrival in Florence comfortable, my equipment safe, and my stay productive; Patrizia Carella, whose smile warmed each of my visits to the Biblioteca; and so many others at the Center who made me feel welcome.

In the U.S., my deep thanks extend to Alexa M. Mason, I Tatti's guardian angel in Cambridge, whose grace, intelligence, and efficiency still make their impact felt; to Dr. Elizabeth Streicher Epstein of the National Gallery of Art, who arranged for my first visit to I Tatti in 1992; to Frederick M. Smith, M.D., friend and colleague, whose help and advice in one frenetic week of work at the villa were invaluable; to David Finn, whose generosity permitted my participation in this project, and whose many accomplishments continue to fill me with much admiration, and some envy; to Paul Gottlieb, Editor-in-Chief of Harry N. Abrams, Inc., whose many courtesies reassured me that there was more than one New York; and to Dr. Elaine M. Stainton, this book's editor, who dismisses my artistic insecurities, returns telephone calls scrupulously, and suffers fools with unfailing patience and humor. My great debt to Barbara Matler Morowitz, for thirty-three years my wife, confidant, and counselor is well known to her, but I reiterate it here, nonetheless.

David Morowitz

Photographing the villa, gardens, and works of art at I Tatti was both a joy and a challenge. I have never seen any place quite like it in the world. There is a sense of perfection in almost every element—the library, the decoration of the rooms, the individual furnishings, the works of art, the gardens, and perhaps most of all, in the scholars who work there. When I began working on the project, I had the pleasure of spending time with the art historians Angelica Rudenstine, John Pope-Hennessy, Kenneth Clark, and Frederick Hartt, all old friends of I Tatti. Through their eyes, and from their many personal recollections, I was given a glimpse of what the villa might have been like when Berenson was there. But I had the feeling that today, Berenson's creation has taken on a life of its own, and has become an evolving institution with a great future, as well as a distinguished past.

I have been privileged to photograph I Tatti at different times of the year over many years through the generosity of Walter Kaiser, whose hospitality and warmth have been for me and my wife among the great treasures of the villa. The selection in this volume from the hundreds of photographs I have taken, together with the excellent photographs by David Morowitz, will, I hope, give readers a glimpse of what it is like to be in this remarkable environment.

I, too, owe a debt of gratitude to all the individuals mentioned by David Morowitz, who were extraordinarily helpful to both of us. I would like to add a special word of thanks to Maurizio Ghiglia, a fine photographer and a good friend, who provided invaluable assistance to me in photographing the paintings in the I Tatti collection.

David Finn

Sculpture in the enclosed garden.
Photo: David Morowitz

Index

Pages in italics refer to illustrations

Editor: Elaine M. Stainton

Designer: Carol A. Robson

Library of Congress Cataloging-in-Publication Data

Weaver, William, 1923–
    A legacy of excellence : the story of Villa I Tatti / by William Weaver.
       p.   cm.
    ISBN 0–8109–3587–2 (clothbound)
    1. Berenson, Bernard, 1865–1959—Homes and haunts—Italy—
Florence. 2. Berenson, Mary, 1864–1945 —Homes and haunts—Italy—
Florence. 3. Berenson, Bernard, 1865–1959—Relations with friends
and associates. 4. Villa I Tatti (Florence, Italy) I. Title.
    N7483. B47W43 1997
    709' .2—dc20   96–31347

Printed and bound in Japan